Bla

A Balanced Discussion
Version 2.0

Healing Racial Divide

C.L. Holley

Information in this book is available as:

Keynote Speech
Corporate Training
Conference Session

Visit SpeakerHolley.com for bookings

Cover photo by Wylly, Suhendra on unsplash.com
Copyright © 2020 - 2021 Charles L Holley

This book is cataloged with the Library of Congress.

V16-09162023

Paperback ISBN-13: 979-8677373954
Hardcover ISBN-13: 979-8790508547
Ebook ASIN: B00Q26U7V8

DEDICATION

To Dad & Mom
(My high school teachers)

Paul and Jeanette Hargrove

In a time of racial unrest and resistance to school integration, you accepted black boys and girls as if we were your own. You gave us love, discipline, and great examples of godly character. You changed the lives of many minorities, including the life of the author of this book. May God bless you and your offspring forever for your unconditional love. I love you both with all my heart.

Reviews

"This work does a masterful job of handling a difficult subject with a tone that is fair, honest, accurate, and not demeaning or condescending to any side of the ongoing racial debate. This is the book for those from both sides who want to understand the issue at its core."

"An Amazing Book - Buy it, read it, learn from it. If I could give this book a thousand stars I would."

"This is a book that welcomes you. It does not declare, pronounce, posit, demand, or do anything of the sort."

"This is a very thought-provoking book. You cannot read this and not be moved by its powerful content, ideas, and stories."

"This is a very eye-opening book and really does make you stop and think."

"There is so much to like about this book. Its non-confrontational approach…"

"Anyone not seeing the truth and wisdom of this book is simply in denial."

"I really enjoyed reading this book! It's a perfect combination of more academic/historic research and telling the author's personal story."

"This book, more than any other I have read, helped me understand the racial divide in the US and gave me ideas on how to improve things."

"What I liked most was the dispassionate balance and sincerity of the arguments made – No propaganda here."

Contents

The Beauty of Colors

Nature presents colors in a brilliant fashion. Have you marveled at the awesome sight of a beautiful rainbow hovering over the glistening waters of a calm sea? Invigorating!

Ever seen the captivating view of a spectacular sunrise or watched in awe at the fascinating mixture of colors as they danced during a slow sunset? Incredible!

Take a beautiful bouquet adorned with different colors, shapes, and sizes of flowers. Lovely!

What makes all these natural sceneries beautiful beyond belief? One word: Colors.

With flowers each color on its own is pretty and can stand alone as a single flower in a vase. However, to create a stunningly beautiful arrangement, one must put different colors, shapes, and sizes together in one vase.

Isn't it strange that in nature sceneries must have different colors to look their best? Nature is built such that no single color can look its best until another color stands beside it—complimenting it—creating that breath taking rainbow of splendor for all the world to see and admire.

It is the same with humans, but this truth is not evident in the racial violence occurring in the United States and around the world. In fact, some humans use colors not to compliment but to compete and even clash. It is the intelligent human who has taken the breath-taking beauty of skin color and turned it into an object of ridicule—even to the point of loathing and hatred.

For example, roses come in different colors, but they all are beautiful. Why have some humans suggested the white rose represents PURITY, the red rose represents LOVE, and the black rose represents DEATH?

It was not the black rose that suggested that ill-advised association. It was humans—those intelligent beings who themselves come in different colors. Unfortunately, many people who admire different colors of nature also disdain certain colors of humans. This flaw is a by-product of racism.

I suppose that is why I cried when I saw the gruesome killing of George Floyd on national media. I wept at the sight of him consistently pleading for mercy, saying, "I can't breathe!" The horrible incident changed me. It shook me to the core of my being. I wondered how we could come so far yet still end up lagging so far behind.

I thought about the progress we have made in education. I spent the first two years of school in a small Negro schoolhouse. We were bused to an all-white school in the early 1970s. That was the beginning of my experience with white kids, and it made me a better person.

I thought about the tremendous progress we have made in social society. When I was small, my parents loved hamburgers and frequented a local restaurant. Because of Jim Crow laws blacks could not go in through the front door. Instead, we walked around the back, stepped over the bushes, carefully avoided the briers, and stood next to the garbage cans that reeked with rotten food. From a small dirty window we ordered, paid, and collected our burgers.

Yes, we have made tremendous strides as a nation and as a people. But it should be clear, especially after the brutal killing of George Floyd, that we have a long way to go before all races achieve true equality.

Therefore, we must come together and have tough talks by getting past two conversation killers: guilt and unforgiveness.

Guilt is a feeling of condemnation that some whites have when discussing racism. It leads to a defensive posture and ultimately to accusations of being blamed for the ills of blacks. Guilt is a sign that the person is not approaching race discussions with the right posture of self-evaluation. Those who have guilt will often Defend, Deflect, and Deny.

For example, a middle-aged Caucasian woman came to a book club event to discuss racism with the author. She came prepared with statistics on various causes of black problems such as abortion, school drop-out, single parent homes, and more. When asked if she also had statistics on how racism affected blacks, she said, "No."

Why did she feel compelled to dig up statistics on everything except racism? Was it to cover her guilt by suggesting racism was not a widespread issue—thereby putting all the blame on blacks themselves? She could have researched and discovered how the post-civil war racist systems of peonage, pig-laws, and black codes decimated black families through mass incarceration, heavy debt, and even murders.

When thousands of black men are taken out of the family and placed in prisons, it creates single family homes and other issues such as poverty and crime. Such occurrences tend to have a long-lasting impact and could affect families for several generations.

Again, all black single parent homes today are not due to racism, but we should acknowledge the toll those racist laws took on black families. To successfully discuss racism, we should not convolute the subject matter, and we should approach the conversation humbly asking three tough questions. What were the historical mindsets and biases toward race? Do I have any of those mindsets and biases? If so, what must I do to change?

This book was not written to heap guilt upon my Caucasian brothers and sisters for the sins of the past. The information in this book about the antebellum south, confederacy, and slave related issues is not provided to hurt, but to help usher in truth that will lead to racial healing.

Unforgiveness is the incorrect posture that some blacks exhibit regarding racial issues. It manifests in anger and frustration when discussing racism with white people. Hard-line-tones and statements such as, "You just don't get it!" tend to shutdown conversations.

These statements create a tense environment where some white people may feel intimidated and incapable to contribute to the subject matter. Instead, blacks should also come humbly into the discussion—being careful with their choice of words and demonstrating patience with others.

I do make a sincere attempt to address racism from a neutral place by providing analysis and constructive suggestions for both blacks and whites.

For non-Christian readers, biblical scriptures are contained in this book with no intentions to proselytize anyone. Their purpose is to connect with Christian readers because, as I point out in a later chapter, racism runs rampant in the Christian church. I hope the presence of scriptures does not hinder your reception of the overall message of the book.

There are four main points shared throughout this book.

One. Racism is not about skin color alone. It is a character sickness with roots that are colorless such as pride, greed, selfishness, and hatred.

Two. ALL people, including blacks, are subject to supremacist, racist, and biased mindsets, attitudes, and conduct. Real life stories and examples of racism committed by some blacks have been added in Chapter Four, White and Black Challenges, to bring more balance to this book.

Three. There are specific challenges that all races need to confront to help heal the racial divide. These suggestions are represented in the Black and White challenges section. However, this section has been expanded to include all races to represent a global call for racial harmony.

Four. This is a book of SELF reflection written to lead you, the reader, into a place of pondering and evaluating yourself as it relates to racial issues. If you choose to leave a review, please include information about your personal racial experiences and growth. In the end, you and I are powerless to change others, but we can change ourselves.

I am convinced racial healing must be approached with 100% engagement from all races. With the heightened social justice awareness, could 2020 be the beginning of true reconciliation for the races not only in America, but around the globe? Will the social justice movement progress beyond a few law modifications and broken promises by those in seats of power?

My Momma was born in the 1920s, survived the great depression, and experienced the humiliation of racism through Jim Crow laws. She only had an eighth grade Negro education. But she often repeated a saying about situations that were difficult to change. She said, "We will see."

We will see if the world is ready to have those uncomfortable conversations about race. We will see if people are willing to be humble and seek racial healing. We will see if each person is willing to look deep within, face the challenges of coming together, and truly work toward racial unity.

I have a firm belief and a constant hope that every race from every corner of the world will come together with love and respect, to reduce racism to the minority, and elevate love to the majority.

Pre-Read Exercise

Please perform this quick exercise before continuing. It will be referenced at the end of the book.

Take a few moments to think about the word America. If needed, close your eyes, and allow any images of people, places, or things that you consider to be American to form in your mind. Write down those things below.

Image:

Image:

Image:

Image:

Image

CHAPTER ONE

Supremacy, Racism, and Bias

The 1950s were tumultuous times in America and especially in my home state of Alabama. The desegregation movement caused racial tensions to reach a boiling point across the country and in our small, desegregated neighborhood. Black and white neighbors who had known each other for years, and even considered themselves friends, were at odds. The residual effects of Jim Crow segregation laws were prevalent.

One day, someone threw a brick through the front window of the small house my family lived in—smashing the glass and ruining a pot of fresh peaches on the kitchen table. My father became furious and threatened to take his gun and go after the culprit, but my mother managed to calm him down and quietly cleaned up the mess.

Within this explosive environment lived people like my parents who were the original odd couple. My mother, Pearl, was extremely quiet, shy, and reserved. She sought to avoid any conflict with whites. Her character was molded from a difficult life. Born in the 1920s, she barely survived the great depression and had experienced the harsh reality of racism and Jim Crow laws.

She had seen what could happen to blacks in the south who got too far out of line—the brutality, shaming, and even death. She was so fearful of conflict that she did not look white people in the eyes when talking to them. She simply offered a "Yes, Sir" and "No, Sir."

However, my father, John, was the complete opposite—loud, angry, and combative. The tough years of backbreaking sharecropping (farming) for little pay and daily discrimination formed a huge racial chip on his shoulder. He had no problem looking white people directly in the eyes and telling them exactly how he felt about the injustices of his day.

In fact, he was known for getting into heated arguments with his white neighbors and wielding a shotgun just inches from their face. A church deacon, he would warn them, "Get out of my yard before I send you to meet Jesus!"

My father was known among whites in the neighborhood as "that uppity crazy ni**er." I describe him as a cross between Martin Luther King, Jr. (who shared his dream of love and unity), Malcolm X (who freed himself by any means necessary), and Mahatma Gandhi (who prayed for his enemies). He was a hardworking man who kept his family fed, clothed, and sheltered. Yet he had a dark side. He could be charming and gentle one minute and extremely violent the next.

Given the times and my father's quick temper, a major confrontation was inevitable. One day, during the early morning hours, a major clash occurred.

As Pearl rocked in her rocking chair, a loud gunshot blast interrupted the peaceful silence. Pearl jumped from her rocking chair and rushed to the window. She looked around the front yard and saw my father as he walked by with his shotgun draped over his shoulder. She also saw a wounded dog scampering down the road as it howled from the pain of a gunshot wound. She held her hands over her panicked heart and tried to decrease its rapid rhythm.

"Oh, God, no!" she exclaimed.

John cursed and complained as he came into the house. "I told that man to keep his damn dog out of my garbage cans!" He scolded. "Maybe he'll learn to tie him up now!"

Pearl gasped for breath and asked, "Oh no, why did you do such a fool thang like that at a time like this? What's gon happen to our kids? What they gon do to us?"

John stared at her and casually walked to the bedroom, put his gun on the dresser, and lay on the bed as if nothing happened. But Pearl was terrified and couldn't stop pacing the floor. She continued to peek out the front window of the tiny house. Minutes later, she saw their neighbor, a large white man, marching down the road. He waved a shotgun and yelled threatening words toward the house.

"You shot my dog, you black bastard!" He screamed. "Just for that, I'm gon kill your family in front of your face, and then I'm gon take care of you!"

Pearl quickly closed the curtains and ran to the room where her kids had huddled in fear. She pulled them close.

"Now listen real good," she said. "If that man gets past me, I want y'all to run out the back, and run as fast as you can. Run to your auntie's house and don't look back!"

In the meantime, John rose from the bed and began searching for shotgun shells as the raging voice of the man grew louder and closer. Pearl positioned herself behind the front door and offered up a quick prayer before facing her enraged neighbor.

When he came within a few yards of the house, Pearl opened the front door and ran toward him. She fell on her knees, stretched out her arms, and begged him not to harm her kids.

He cocked the shotgun and pointed it at her.

"Please, Sir," she pleaded. "Pease don't do this! I'm awful sorry 'bout your dog, but please don't kill my kids over it!"

She crawled toward him, grabbed his ankles, and continued to beg for mercy.

"Who does that ni**er think he is anyway to shoot my dog?" He yelled. "I aim to teach him a lesson he ain't gon never forget! Now, let me go!"

He tried to shake Pearl from his ankles as he continued to force his way toward the front door. He dragged her along the ground with every forceful step, but she held on with all her tiny might, and continued to beg with each yard he gained. She began to pray out loud. "Lord Jesus, please help me! Lord. Please don't let him do this! Lord, I'm begging you, Jesus! Touch his heart Lord! Please touch his heart!"

Seconds later, the strangest thing happened. He stopped and looked down at her—a poor black woman wrapped around his ankles, begging not for her life, but for the lives of her children. He looked at the front window of the tiny house and saw the terrified eyes of several small children.

Seconds later he lowered the shotgun and said, "I'm gon do what you asked. But I'm not doing it for him. I'm doing it for you and for your kids. Now let me go."

Pearl slowly loosened her grip on his ankles and raised up on her knees as she continued to look down, and said, "Thank you kindly, Sir. Thank you kindly."

He placed the shotgun on his shoulder, turned, and walked back down the road.

Pearl didn't get up after he left. Instead, she stayed on the ground and released tears of gratitude for the terror that was averted. She continued to pray and thank God for sparing their lives. When she recounted the story to us, she always referred to the incident as a miracle from God.

Supremacy, Racism, and Bias

Words mean different things to different people. Before racial unity can take place, there must be agreement on the meaning of three words: Supremacy, Racism, and Unconscious Bias.

Racial Supremacy

The state or condition of being superior to all others in authority, power, or status. (Dictionary)

Racial supremacy is a flawed philosophy that promotes one's race as superior. This involves embracing the notion that people of one race should control the power structure and enjoy certain privileges of society that are unavailable to others.

Supremacists tend to have a strong belief that different races cannot live together in harmony, respect, and love. After all, that would require equality between races. Instead, they only believe in dominance—that one race will always dominate the other. That is why they focus on ruling the power structure and have a constant fear of other races securing freedom, wealth, and political capital. Their motto is usually, "Dominate or be dominated."

A person with a supremacist mindset may use words or phrases such as:

"Go back where you came from!" (This is my country.)

"They should serve us." (Others are inferior servants.)

"He or she is just that Negro ..."
(Maximize race and minimize accomplishments)

For example, during the early stages of the civil rights movement, several leaders in high places often privately referred to Martin Luther King, Jr. as "that Negro Preacher." The supremacist mindset tends to refer to race first because this is how they determine value and worth.

Years ago, I worked with a white man who believed in white supremacy. This person did not keep his beliefs a secret and constantly made racially insensitive comments about black issues. One day, I was having a casual conversation with a group of coworkers about an upcoming Martin Luther King Jr. Day celebration.

He butted into the conversation and retorted, "Why would I want to celebrate Martin Luther King Day? I'd rather celebrate the man who shot him."

He was eventually fired for verbally attacking his black manager's white wife. The supremacist hated interracial relationships and occasionally made derogatory statements about his manager's blended marriage.

Adolf Hitler, the German Nazi responsible for the Jewish Holocaust and killing of around six million Jews during World War II, believed in this same flawed philosophy. Unfortunately, supremacy is embraced by some people and groups in America today and is not limited to the Caucasian race. Some blacks also believe in supremacy.

The supremacy philosophy is condemned by the Christian faith and is not supported by any credible scientific findings.

> *"And he made from one man every nation of mankind to live on all the face of the earth, having determined allotted periods and the boundaries of their dwelling place,.." (Acts 17:26)*
>
> *"For God shows no partiality." (Romans 2:11)*

Racism

Prejudice, discrimination, or antagonism directed against a person or people based on their membership of a particular racial or ethnic group, typically one that is a minority or marginalized. The belief that different races possess distinct characteristics, abilities, or qualities, especially so as to distinguish them as inferior or superior to one another. (Dictionary)

Racism is a belief that may not necessarily subscribe to supremacy but advocates racial separation due to the "purity" of each race. This line of thinking opposes interracial marriages, interracial children, blended families, and other forms of integration such as schools, neighborhoods, businesses, and more.

Racism often employs and supports various methods of separation both covert or overt and lawful or unlawful. A person with a racist mindset may use such words and phrases as:

"Y'all need to stick with your kind." (Stay with your race.)

"What are you doing here?" (You don't belong here.)

"Let us have our stuff and y'all have yours." (Separate)

All people who subscribe to supremacy ideals also believe in the separation of races. But not all people who hold racist beliefs do so because of supremacy. Both have the same goal in mind of strict racial separation.

When I was in college as a student-athlete, I met a white female-athlete who had been born and raised in a very racist town. Whenever our conversations turned to race-related issues, she was quick to say she did not believe in racial supremacy, but she did believe races should stay with their own kind. When I pressed her to explain why, she always went back to the familiar refrain of, "That's just the way I was raised."

The 1896 United States Supreme Court ruling of separate but equal was based, in part, on this belief. The court ruled that racial segregation was constitutional and that separate public facilities for blacks and whites was allowed on the condition that both facilities were equal in quality. That ruling gave power and legality to racist laws such as state and local mandated segregation laws in the south known as Jim Crow laws. There is always a pattern of behavior with supremacy and racism beliefs.

A lack of sympathy or empathy: The inability to feel compassion or sorrow for someone who experienced tragedy due to their race. The person may say, "I don't care."

A lack of sincere compliments: The inability to say anything good about a race, and any attempts to compliment result in side-swipe comments meant to belittle or degrade a race.

A lack of defense: The unwillingness to defend those who are mistreated, attacked, or have experienced injustice due to their race.

The Christian faith condemns racism, and it is not supported by credible scientific findings.

> *"Truly I understand that God shows no partiality, but in every nation anyone who fears him and does what is right is acceptable to him." (Acts 10:34-35 ESV)*

Unconscious Bias

Prejudice in favor of or against one thing, person, or group compared with another, usually in a way considered to be unfair. (Dictionary)

Unconscious biases are those deep subconscious thoughts and opinions developed over time and through a variety of means. They can stem from a combination of learning (or lack thereof), family tradition, and social activity to name a few. These biased thoughts and opinions are usually not based on solid research or accurate information.

All humans have bias. It is not a question of if, but a question of in what areas and how much. Because bias tends to develop over time, it is possible to harbor a racial bias for many years or even a lifetime. But there is good news about a bias. What is learned can be unlearned if the person is willing to release the bias and embrace the truth.

Supremacists and racists tend to tightly maintain their racial biases and make those untruths the foundation of their beliefs. They defend and protect these false notions and conveniently find excuses to reject the truth. They may constantly say, "I'm just standing up for what I believe."

Yet, when challenged to support their belief with the moral truth of the biblical scriptures or scientific findings, they cannot. Instead, their refrain may be, "That's just what I believe."

A bias belief usually sets the stage for unfair privileges such as preferential treatment or avoidance of negative occurrences due to race. ANY race can have unfair privileges. Regardless of your race, answer the following questions to determine if you have benefited from unfair racial privilege.

Have you been followed or "closely monitored" while shopping?

Have you had a negative police encounter on more than one occasion?

Have you been called or referred to indirectly by a racial slur?

Have you been denied access to services or products due to race?

Have you lived in a neighborhood where you were not welcomed because of your race?

If you answered Yes to two or more questions, in my opinion, you have not benefited from racial privilege. But if you answered No to three or more questions, I believe you have benefited from bias that produces racial privilege.

Some signs of extreme bias thinking are:

Roller Coaster Emotions: Going rapidly between emotions such as fear, hatred, and sadness when contemplating events in society.

Unbalanced Thinking: Minimizing the seriousness of covid-19 while maximizing the seriousness of other diseases.

Acceptance of Unfounded Beliefs: Accepting conspiracy theories, plots, and rumors that have no credible sources.

Here are some popular racial biases toward African Americans according to the Ferris State University website:

(https://www.ferris.edu/htmls/news/jimcrow/links/essays/vcu.htm)

Sambo

"One of the most enduring stereotypes in American history is that of the Sambo (Boskin, 1986). This pervasive image of a simple-minded, docile black man dates back at least as far as the colonization of America. The Sambo stereotype flourished during the reign of slavery in the United States. In fact, the notion of the "happy slave" is the core of the Sambo caricature."

Jim Crow

The stereotyping of African Americans was brought to the theatrical stage with the advent of the blackface minstrel (Engle, 1978). Beginning in the early 19th century, white performers darkened their faces with burnt cork, painted grotesquely exaggerated white mouths over their own, donned woolly black wigs and took the stage to entertain society. The character they created was Jim Crow. This "city dandy" was the northern counterpart to the southern "plantation darky," the Sambo (Engle, 1978 p. 3).

The Savage

Movies were, and still are, a powerful medium for the transmission of stereotypes. Early silent movies such as "The Wooing and Wedding of a Coon" in 1904, "The Slave" in 1905, "The Sambo Series" 1909-1911 and "The Nigger" in 1915 offered existing stereotypes through a fascinating new medium (Boskin, 1986). The premiere of "Birth of a Nation" during the reconstruction period in 1915 marked the change in emphasis from the happy Sambo and the pretentious and inept Jim Crow stereotypes to that of the Savage.

The Mammy

The Mammy was a large, independent woman with pitch-black skin and shining white teeth (Jewell, 1993). She wore a drab calico dress and head scarf and lived to serve her master and mistress. The Mammy understood the value of the white lifestyle. The stereotype suggests that she raised the "massa's" children and loved them dearly, even more than her own.

Aunt Jemimah

The stereotype of Aunt Jemimah evolved out of the Mammy image (Jewell, 1993). She differs from Mammy in that her duties were restricted to cooking. It was through Aunt Jemimah that the association of the African American woman with domestic work, especially cooking, became fixed in the minds of society. As a result, hundreds of Aunt Jemimah collectibles found their way into the American kitchens.

Sapphire

Sapphire was a stereotype solidified through the hit show "Amos 'n' Andy" (Jewell, 1993). This profoundly popular series began on the radio in 1926 and developed into a television series, ending in the 1950s (Boskin, 1986). This cartoon show depicted the Sapphire character as a bossy, headstrong woman who was engaged in an ongoing verbal battle with her husband, Kingfish (Jewell, 1993). Sapphire possessed the emotional makeup of the Mammy and Aunt Jemimah combined.

Jezebelle

The final female stereotype is Jezebelle, the harlot. This image of the "bad Black girl" represented the undeniable sexual side of African American women (Jewell, 1993). The traditional

Jezebelle was a light-skinned, slender Mulatto girl with long straight hair and small features. She more closely resembled the European ideal for beauty than any pre-existing images.

B.O.B (Black on Bottom) Race Messaging

If you live in America, you may have heard of the ugly racist incident that occurred among several city council leaders living in Los Angeles, California. A group of Hispanic council leaders berated a black child--one of them calling the child a "monkey." Unfortunately, incidents like that are not new, just caught on video or audio.

In fact, those incidents are hundreds of years old, dating back to antebellum period where black slaves were constantly cast as the "bottom" or lowest of all races. In any society, slaves were always considered as the bottom in terms of social standing, rights, and worth. Therefore, in America, a nation that utilized slavery during its early formation, blacks were often portrayed in a variety of media messaging (papers, books, signs, posters, silent movies, etc.) as the worst of races.

A Hispanic friend confessed this to me when we discussed race. "To some Hispanics," she said, "blacks are the worst of races. It is said to make sure you do not date or marry a black."

B.O.B messaging are those communications that say, suggest, or imply blacks are inferior, violent, dumb, or any other negative association that suggests they are the worst of races. American media was filled with those messages, especially after the civil war and during the height of the white supremacy movement.

All other races were exposed to that messaging as well. Therefore, it is not surprising to hear some Hispanics, Natives,

Asians, Jews, Arabs, and Whites regard blacks as the worst. Blacks have been subjected to that messaging for over 400 years.

Here are some names I have personally heard blacks called:

Monkeys
Apes
Baboons
Gorillas
Coons
Crows
Black-birds
and Dogs.

An older family member who grew up subjected to constant racism in the south, told me a heartbreaking story of a racist encounter he had as a young grocery store worker in the 1960s. As he stocked the shelves with food items, a white man and his young son walked by. The boy pointed at him and said, "Hey Daddy, look at that monkey! And he don't even have a tail!"

The father and son laughed and walked away.

But concerning the bottom mentality, a person would have to be a supremacist or a separatist to believe there is a bottom. Only racists believe in racial hierarchies where the notion is, *someone must be on top and someone must be on bottom.* A person who believes in racial equality does not believe there is a racial top or bottom--just different people where some are good, and some are bad.

Stereotypes today

Although much has changed since the days of Sambo, Jim Crow, the Savage, Mammy, Aunt Jemimah, Sapphire and Jezebelle, it can be argued convincingly that similar stereotypes of African Americans exist in 1998. Author Joseph Boskin states that "...there should be little doubt that aspects of Sambo live on in the White mind and show through the crevices of American culture in subtle and sophisticated ways" (Boskin, 1986, p. 15). However, the predominant modern stereotypes are the violent, brutish African American male and the dominant, lazy African American female - the Welfare Mother (Peffley Hurwitz & Sniderman, 1997).

My motto is, He who controls the media, controls the minds. If you are white, you may wonder, "With all these stereotypes, how can I possibly avoid them all in my engagements with African Americans?"

That is a legitimate question. I don't believe whites can avoid all of them. That is why a humble attitude is needed from whites and blacks, to gently give correction, and gently receive correction. However, just knowing them puts you at an advantage over other whites who do not know.

As mentioned, all humans formulate engrained biases in multiple areas such as race, gender, and others. There are multiple sources of bias including social media, news outlets, special interest groups, and even family and friends. Some biases can be obvious, and others hidden in the suggestive messaging of audio, images, and text.

I once worked with a black guy who shared an incident of racial bias. When he was in college, he lived with his parents in a large, nice home not far from the college campus, and often cut the grass.

One day, several of his white college mates drove by and saw him cutting the grass. When he saw them days later, one of them said, "I saw you the other day cutting someone's yard. I did not know you cut grass for a living. Whose grass were you cutting?"

He replied, "Mine. I live there."

He said his college mates had difficulty believing he lived in that gorgeous house. That was an obvious case of racial bias.

Do you have racial bias? If so, that alone does not make you a supremacist or racist. Like millions of other people in the world, you need to confess those biases, reject them, and embrace the truth. Racial biases are condemned by the Christian faith and are proven to exist by social and scientific case studies.

"Do not judge by appearances, but judge with right judgment." (John 7:24 ESV)

Discrimination
The unjust or prejudicial treatment of different categories of people or things, especially on the grounds of race, age, or sex; recognition and understanding of the difference between one thing and another. (Dictionary)

All three of the previously mentioned terms of supremacy, racism, and unconscious bias tend to result in various acts of discrimination. These unfair and sometimes unlawful acts can manifest in the areas of:

Housing: Reserving a neighborhood for a certain race by preventing access to quality and affordable housing.

Education: Systematically placing roadblocks to quality educational systems to keep access for certain races limited.

Healthcare: Failing to act on or pass healthcare laws that will ensure equal access to doctors, testing, and medication.

Voting: Systematically placing roadblocks to voting and strategically devising methods to avoid counting legitimate votes.

Employment: Utilizing unfair selective practices of choosing or rejecting potential employment candidates based on race.

These discriminatory mindsets and acts often lead to disenfranchisement, disengagement, and huge disadvantages for people of all races, and particularly for minorities in America. Sadly, these acts are often coordinated and calculated between authority figures on different levels of power—making it systemic in nature.

In 1969, my parents lived under many discriminatory practices and laws in our area. They loved hamburgers, and on my father's payday, often stopped by a small restaurant not far from our house. Even though they paid the same price as everyone else, they could not go in through the front door. They had to go around the back, step through the bushes and briers, and stand next to the garbage dump as they ordered from a small dirty window in the back of the building.

What type of message do you think that situation sent to my parents and other black people? The message was clear: Black people are not as important as white people and certainly not equal.

The Christian faith firmly condemns discrimination, and it has been proven to exist by numerous social and scientific case studies.

> *"My brothers, show no partiality as you hold the faith in our Lord Jesus Christ, the Lord of glory. 2 For if a man wearing a gold ring and fine clothing comes into your assembly, and a poor man in shabby clothing also comes in, 3 and if you pay attention to the one who wears the fine clothing and say, "You sit here in a good place," while you say to the poor man, "You stand over there," or, "Sit down at my feet," 4 have you not then made distinctions among yourselves and become judges with evil thoughts?" (James 2:1-4 ESV)*

We can summarize them in the following chart. All three beliefs lead to the act of discrimination, but there are different reasons and rationale for acts of discrimination.

	Superior?	Separation?	Discriminate?
Supremacy:	Yes	Yes	Yes
Racism:	No	Yes	Yes
Uncon Bias:	No	No	Yes

The Four Pillars of Racism

Four hundred years of anything is an extremely long time. Yet, for African Americans, the perpetuation of supremacy, racism, and discrimination has survived the centuries of slavery, Black

Codes, and Jim Crow laws. They have even endured despite the periods of spiritual awakening in the United States.

How do these evil practices continue to pass from century to century and from generation to generation? I want to share what I call the Four Pillars of Racism. I believe these character flaws and acts are pillars—foundations that allow and encourage supremacy and racism to flourish in their many forms.

Ungodly Pride-Arrogance

Ungodly pride is the audacity to consider oneself more valuable or important than others. It is a major reason racism continues to be perpetuated from generation to generation. Ungodly pride is widely considered in the Christian faith to be the original sin of Satan (the devil)—wanting to elevate his self-importance above the Most High God of Heaven and Earth (Isaiah 14:12-16).

The desire to be first is not necessarily bad unless it is at the cost of vilifying or displacing another to make oneself appear better. People plagued with pride and arrogance are boasters of their own abilities. They extremely exaggerate their potential, worth, and acts of compassion and mercy. They scream, "I want to be FIRST! Put the spotlight directly on ME!"

Therefore, if pride plots to be first, logically, someone must be second, third, and so forth. Once pride establishes a hierarchy, arrogance takes over to make sure everyone knows who is superior (first) and who is inferior (last). These two monsters often work in conjunction to create systemic injustice and unfair practices to keep people in the lowest state of existence.

No wonder pride and arrogance top the list of seven things God hates.

There are six things that the LORD hates,

seven that are an abomination to him:

haughty eyes, a lying tongue,

and hands that shed innocent blood,

a heart that devises wicked plans,

feet that make haste to run to evil,

a false witness who breathes out lies,

and one who sows discord among brothers.

(Proverbs 6:16-19).

Fear-Hatred

Fear is often a precursor to the manifestation of hateful acts against others. People can become fearful of others' achievements in a manner that casts a negative spotlight on themselves. In these cases, fearful folks can express their hatred by attacking or even killing others.

An example of this is the 1921 Tulsa Oklahoma race riots where whites attached a town of successful blacks, known as black Wall Street, killing many and burning down their houses and businesses.

It has been referred to as the single worst incident of racial violence in American history. Estimates of around 800 people were hospitalized and around 6,000 blacks placed in internment facilities for days. Between 75 and 300 people were killed.

The horrible incident was said to occur after a young white girl accused a young black man of assault. But no matter the cause, how could violence have escalated to such a level? Could it be that many white residents may have had envy, jealously, and fear in their hearts toward those successful blacks?

The common theme of fear and hatred is, "If they gain, we lose." In the slave era it was, "If they gain their freedom, we lose our servants, our economy, and our elevated status in society."

Fear focuses on making situations better for oneself while faith focuses on making situations better for others.

Anytime hatred manifests, always look below the expressions and acts of violence and ask the question, "What was that person afraid of?"

There is a real fear among some of our white brothers and sisters of becoming the minority race in America. There are several population studies and estimates that suggest this will happen by 2045. Perhaps some worry about retribution and revenge for hundreds of years of injustice and ill-treatment. Perhaps they wonder whether they will be forced to walk a trail of tears as the Native Americans were forced to do after the Indian Removal Act.

Perhaps they wonder about becoming second-class citizens and losing their privileged status. Will they lose the power, control, and the advantages that accompany being white?

All these concerns are understandable. But the collective body of races should offer a comforting, "Not on my watch."

The goal of civil rights and social justice is not revenge or retribution of wrongs, but to ensure there is no race that suffers injustice—including the white race. We should fight racism not to make another race the minority, but to make supremacy, racism, and bias minority beliefs and practices.

Although racism will always exist in our world, the stronger principles and practices of true equality will also exist. And after fighting the good fight of equal justice, at the end of the day, we can repeat the wise words of Martin Luther King, Jr.,

> *"The arc of the moral universe is long, but it bends toward justice."*

Lies-Ignorance

In the Christian faith, ignorant does not mean incapable of learning. Rather, it means devoid of truth. Unfortunately, we live in a world filled with lies, misinformation, and stereotypes that permeate social media platforms leading to inaccurate conclusions and false beliefs. Adding to this problem is the fact that most people will not test or dig for truth but will accept the first rendition of false information that appears.

Although the Christian faith says much about the danger of lies and the importance of testing everything, fake data seems to constantly win airtime and attention.

How does one navigate the complex sea of rapidly changing information? What is true and what is false?

It has become more important to follow up and closely examine all information including that emanating from television, radio, and online sources. Asking the commonsense questions of who, what, and why will aid in dissecting convoluted data and help one arrive at the truth.

However, a person must want the truth and not become satisfied with the first report that surfaces. That means a willingness to research and examine what is necessary to arrive at a sound conclusion.

Are you testing your sources of information? Are you comparing at least two diverse and credible media outlets—contrasting them to determine accuracy and misinformation? If not, you could be aiding in spreading false information.

Passivity

The civil rights movement never ended. Yes, there were successes, but the overall goal, to change the hearts of some of our white brothers and sisters, never reached fruition.
From slavery to civil rights, there have always been three places to stand:

1. Supremacist/Racist: Those who seek to exercise power and control over others.

2. Passivist: A safe place for those who don't want to risk anything and are too comfortable with their life.

3. Activist: A place of risk, sacrifice, and vocal support for equal justice for all people.

The passivist is the silent person who believes racism is wrong but has no desire to become an activist for fear of losing their many privileges and comforts of life. They may have remorse for injustice and even express it in private to the ones who are disadvantaged, but they will never rise and challenge the system of racism nor those in seats of power.

Therefore, racism and injustice continue under their watch because they make no serious effort to oppose it. They may surmise, "I don't like what's happening to others, but I love my lifestyle too much to risk losing it. Why should I get involved?"

Have you ever wondered what you would have done during the height of the civil rights movement in 1950s and 1960s? Your answer is, "Whatever you are doing right now."

Along this civil rights continuum, where are you? Are you speaking out in multiple ways through multiple platforms? Are you supporting various equal justice initiatives? Are you pushing back against those in power who are enacting and supporting injustice by peacefully marching and demonstrating? Are you involved in the voting process by registering voters and voting?

If you are doing none of these things, you may be sitting in the seat of the passivist and unwilling to risk anything for the wellbeing of others. Is that really where you belong? The roots of racism tree sum up the four pillars of racism. We will discuss the tree in detail toward the end of the book.

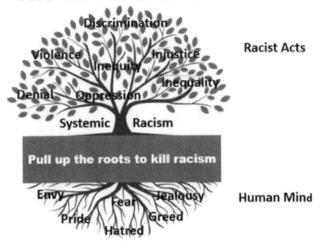

One: Self-Evaluation & Discussion

Who or what were the major racial influencers in your life?

Do you believe in racial supremacy or separation? Why or why not?

Do you have some unconscious bias regarding certain races? If so, where did it come from?

What other points would you want to group-discuss in this chapter?

CHAPTER TWO

SYSTEMIC RACISM

I t was 1984, my first year in college, and the white librarian's behavior shocked me. I applied for a job at the on-campus library. I was fortunate to attend on an athletic scholarship but still needed work to make ends meet. I completed the job application and questionnaire and handed them to the elderly Caucasian woman managing the library. That's when it happened.

I was neat, sat up straight in the chair, and spoke clearly and politely. She seemed pleasantly surprised as she read my answers on the questionnaire. I didn't know why. After all, the questionnaire was very simple middle school-level math. It contained book numbers that needed to be listed in the order they would be shelved. I thought it was a piece of cake, but she reacted as if I just properly factored a college-level, multi-layered algebra equation with three possible solutions. Okay, I'm exaggerating a bit, but not by much.

"Wow!" She exclaimed. "You did it! You can shelve books!" She continued to congratulate me, but I thought her behavior was demeaning. I wanted to ask her, "Why are you surprised that I can do something so simple?"

I didn't ask, but I often wondered about her reaction. I didn't know her past or her experiences with other blacks, but I was deeply offended that she thought so little of my abilities. Perhaps her reaction wasn't due to my race at all—but that was my perception.

If her reaction was due to a negative racial perception, I would address the issue by showing her I was capable of much more than she imagined. That's how negative perceptions should be addressed—by doing the very opposite of what they state—not by attacking the person holding them.

To be honest, all races have negative perceptions to contend with. Whites are unjustly perceived to be religious hypocrites, untrustworthy, and racists. Jews are unfairly perceived as being stingy. Hispanics are wrongfully perceived to be in the country illegally and often characterized as drug dealers and hit men. Blacks are untruthfully perceived as being dependent on the government, violent, crime plagued, and uneducated.

Perception is dangerous because it is created by taking a molehill and forming a mountain. It uses a small amount of data concerning a few and applies it to all people of a race.

All races have their work cut out for them in terms of tearing down negative perceptions. If the perception is religious hypocrisy, people must prove it wrong by being true to their faith and avoiding judging or condemning others. If the perception is racism, people must strive to treat others in the manner they would want to be treated. If the perception is violence or crime plagued, people must present themselves in a peaceful manner and follow the law.

The way to change negative perception is by proving it wrong—one person at a time. I'm striving every day of my life to prove every negative perception about blacks to be inaccurate. Many of my white friends are doing the same for their race. I realize no matter what I do or accomplish, someone will always harbor negative perceptions about my race and me. There is nothing I can do about those persons. Their hatred has blinded them to the truth and to reality.

However, I can change the minds of those who are open to change and willing to see me, not as a black person, but simply as a person. What are you doing to counter the negative perceptions about you and your race?

✳✳✳

Systemic Racism

The Atlantic slave trade was an elaborate system comprised of major and minor players—all filling their roles and working toward one common goal—enslaving Africans. The role of capturing or pirating blacks was filled by African war lords, tribal leaders, and Europeans who confiscated blacks using various methods of wars, raids, pirating, and more.

After collection, the slaves had to be stored someplace convenient to await purchase and transport. Some blacks were marched in chains from inner Africa to the coast, a journey that could be several hundred miles, and ended at a holding place close to the coast.

The purchasers, European slave traders, arrived at the holding place, bought the slaves, and gathered them into slave ships headed for the Americas and other locations in the west.

The system of capture and transportation had many moving parts and some entities even worked in competition. By the time slavery ended in America, it is estimated that between 10 million and 12 million Africans were shipped during the Atlantic slave trade. That astonishing number of people could not have been captured and transported without the system of entrapment, storage, and transport. Enslavement for the Americas had become systemic.

Systemic racism, or institutional discrimination, is embedded as normal practice within a system, society, or organization. When the African slaves arrived on the shores of the Americas, they passed from one system, the slave providers, to another system, the plantation slave purchasers. Southern confederate states had their own system to purchase, recondition and retrain, punish, or even kill slaves without negative repercussions. And it was all legal. It was systemic.

After the South lost the civil war, most of that systemic racist infrastructure was declared unlawful with the passing and ratification of the thirteenth amendment to the constitution. It outlawed slavery and involuntary servitude in America. Here is the text:

> *"Neither slavery nor involuntary servitude, except as a punishment for crime whereof the party shall have been duly convicted, shall exist within the United States, or any place subject to their jurisdiction."*
>
> *(Thirteenth Amendment Section 1 – December 6th 1865)*

Most agree that southern slavery was systemic, but the release of slaves into a free society did not end systemic racism. Those who continued to support supremacy and racism, and feared integration with blacks, did not give up on controlling and limiting blacks even after the law declared them free members of American society.

Supremacists and racists needed other methods to rein in the freedom and progress of their former slaves. Just as they had done during slavery, some people wanted to develop ways to keep former African slaves impoverished, uneducated, and politically powerless. Thus, the first major systemic move was invented almost immediately after the civil war: the peonage system.

Systemic Justice Discrimination: Mass Black Incarceration

Although involuntary slavery and servitude had been outlawed by the thirteenth amendment to the constitution, the text of the amendment left an opening for supremacists and racists to take advantage of blacks. The words, "Neither slavery nor involuntary servitude except as punishment for a crime ..." provided the opening needed to conduct mass incarceration of blacks.

Under the peonage system, former slaveholding states of the South developed legislation to support forced labor. The laws made it possible for employers to induce or deceive people into signing contracts to work as repayment for their debts or to avoid court fines.

Also, prisoners convicted of crimes could be leased out to private or governmental organizations for labor as a form of payment. Some of the old chain gangs are examples of peonage labor. With private companies profiting off the cheap prison labor, more prisoners meant more profits for the company and the state leaser, and the newly freed blacks made perfect targets for prisoners. Peonage existed in the South and the North because of the fallen economy after the war. Some whites also fell into peonage, but blacks were incarcerated at significantly higher levels.

Numerous people were hired as law enforcement with the specific assignment to find reasons to arrest blacks. Some reasons ranged from petty crimes (loitering) to ridiculous violations (pig laws), and when blacks were convicted and sentenced to prison, they were deceived or forced into signing forced labor contracts.

Sometimes some local business owners took advantage of blacks and paid their court fees in return for working to pay off the debt. Otherwise, they were sent to prison to work as convict labor. Many, unable to read and write, had no idea they were marking an "X" on paper to work for the rest of their lives often for a fabricated crime.

Peonage was the perfect solution for those who feared free blacks and wanted to keep them under control while profiting off black labor. Peonage and other so called "Black Code" laws, effectively transported large numbers of blacks from the slave fields to the prison or made them heavily indebted to whites as laborers. Most blacks were kept impoverished, politically powerless, and most of all unable to take full advantage of their newfound freedom.

Although peonage was outlawed by Congress in 1867, it was not enforced to the letter of the law. Thus, the practice continued to operate and flourish. Other forms of peonage included sharecropping where landowners often gave blacks loans in return for their work in the fields. The loans were to be repaid at harvest season when the crops were turned into cash. My father was a sharecropper.

But some landowners cheated blacks who were still struggling to read and write and were not financially aware of where they stood in terms of paying off the debt.

Different forms of peonage existed until it was finally outlawed in 1942 by President Franklin D. Roosevelt. Wikipedia states this of peonage system of convict leasing:

> *"It was a form of bondage distinctly different from that of the antebellum South in that for most men, and the relatively few women drawn in, this slavery did not last a lifetime and did not automatically extend from one generation to the next. But it was nonetheless slavery – a system in which armies of free men, guilty of no crimes and entitled by law to freedom, were compelled to labor without compensation, were repeatedly bought and sold, and were forced to do the bidding of white masters through the regular application of extraordinary physical coercion."* (Writer Douglas A. Blackmon 2008 p.4)

Unfair systemic racism in the judicial systems did not end with the outlawing of peonage. Sometimes, laws created unintentional consequences of mass incarcerations and undue burdens upon African Americans and other minorities.

The so called "War on Drugs" act passed in 1986, aimed at cracking down on drug users, was intended to catch and incarcerate high-level drug dealers, but instead disparately affected minorities at the lower levels of the drug trade. According to Wikipedia, between 1986 and 1997, federal drug prisoners quintupled with 74% of those convicted being minority low-level drug offenders.

There are some who believe that some architects of the law knew exactly what would happen to minorities. However, some supporters of the law were African Americans and those who supported minority advancement. Therefore, the negative consequences that destroyed many minority families was likely unsuspected by those supporters.

Other unfair practices such as excessive judicial sentencing, stop and frisk, arrest quotas, and police brutality, all combine to create a series of systems designed to disempower minorities—which was the same purpose of slavery.

Systemic Housing Discrimination

President Franklin D Roosevelt's New Deal program increased housing availability for whites, not necessarily for blacks. In fact, the term "redlining" was developed from the discriminatory practices of the Federal Housing Authority at that time. The FHA mapped major metropolitan areas to determine where it was safe to insure mortgages.

Those maps contained red color codes which meant it was too risky to insure. These red codes were located where blacks lived or lived nearby. This enabled whites to have a greater advantage, in terms of equity, than African Americans.

But redlining didn't only happen in the housing sector; it happened in banking, insurance, and healthcare with the denial of services or the charging of exorbitant fees and prices.

Strategically locating low-income housing in areas or neighborhoods with little to no opportunities for social or economic growth is also a systemic practice. When there is an absence of good schools, job opportunities, healthcare services, banks, and other vital entities for healthy communities, people tend to remain in poverty or even sink below that level falling prey to homelessness or even criminal activity.

In some cases, housing discrimination was not a secret. It was even written in government manuals. According to the online article A 'Forgotten History' on How the US Government Segregated America, by Terry Gross, May 2017, she writes:

It was in something called the Underwriting Manual of the Federal Housing Administration, which said that 'incompatible racial groups should not be permitted to live in the same communities.' Meaning that loans to African Americans could not be insured.

The Underwriting Manual of the Federal Housing Administration recommended that highways would be a good way to separate African American from white neighborhoods.

The same article records one development where the FHA refused to go ahead with the building project during World War II unless the developer built a 6-foot-high wall separating his development from a nearby African American neighborhood.

As I wrote this book, in 2020, federal charges were levied against a housing authority of a certain city in the United States—charging it with years of racism by steering blacks away from prominent locations in favor of whites. These types of systemic practices in housing have barred blacks from gaining wealth from the equity in good homes in good neighborhoods—putting many of them behind the curve in wealth equality.

Systemic Employment Discrimination

There is concrete evidence about employment discrimination against African Americans that is backed by history, reports, and many case studies. Historical accounts of blacks subjected to horrible work conditions (prison labor, chain gangs, Memphis sanitation workers, etc.), are well known and well documented.

Gainful employment is extremely important in America because other areas of human life are often determined by the quality of one's occupation. High quality jobs, those with residual income and job security, can lead to the ability to live in high-quality neighborhoods, attend high quality schools, secure a university education, and receive quality healthcare because most people in America receive healthcare through their employers.

Therefore, the effects of employment discrimination reach far beyond the economic impact and well into the educational and healthcare arenas. The importance of making quality jobs accessible to minorities and others who may have a financial disadvantage is crucial to creating and maintaining a healthy and balanced economy.

The American history of employment discrimination from the Black Codes, Jim Crow, and unfair governmental practices, have negatively impacted blacks, other minorities, and even poor and disenfranchised whites.

An online article from Catholic Bishops entitled, Racism and Employment, 2018, stated:

"In 2017 the Harvard University Business School Review documented that hiring discrimination against African Americans was still a reality—and did not decline in the past 25 years. The authors note that despite a growing concern with diversity, "subtle forms of racial

> *stereotypes" in the workplace and "unconscious bias" have shown little change:..."*
>
> *(Open wide Our Hearts, United States Conference of Catholic Bishops, 2018)*

The great lesson here is that people can always find ways around laws. When employers are determined to side-step or ignore equality laws, where there is a will, there is a way. The only foolproof way to end employment discrimination is to change the heart and perception of those who continually engage in the practice. But that does not discount the need for laws and policies to improve equality.

Systemic Location and Healthcare Discrimination

Where a person lives and the condition in which he or she lives can determine the health and wellbeing of not only that individual but other members of the family. And those effects can linger from generation to generation.

During southern slavery, most slave owners lived in comfortable and sometimes very elegant homes, usually situated on the choice part of the property. In contrast, the owner's slaves, except for house Negros, usually lived in tiny run-down shacks situated on less valuable land—separated a fair distance from the master's living quarters.

Slaves, despite their high economic value, lived in deplorable conditions, worked from sunup till sundown, and had little to no access to healthcare. In addition, they were prevented from learning and made dependent upon the slave owner for the necessities of life such as food, clothing, and shelter. The women delivered children who were birthed into the same cycle of hopelessness and despair.

Can you see how location, condition, and lack of necessities can determine a person and a family's wellbeing? Some arrogantly insist that black folks need to pull themselves up by their bootstraps. But how can that happen with those black folks who do not have a pair of boots?

In an online article entitled, The Environment that Racism Built: The Impact of Place on Maternal and Infant Health, 2018, Rejane Frederick writes:

The reality in this nation is that while people can self-regulate some aspects of their health–such as by following the practices listed above—many other factors that determine health are beyond individual control. These factors include the environments in which people are born, live, learn, work, and play.

As studies have shown, these longstanding inequities are centrally caused by racism—a system of power that unjustly hoards vital, life-building opportunities and resources for a category of people who are artificially deemed as racially superior, while disempowering and denying those assets to groups devalued as racially inferior.

The displacement of Native Americans—The Trail of Tears— is a great example of the colonial practice of preserving prime real estate for whites only. In 1838 and 1839, as part of the Indian Removal Act, the US government forced Cherokee Natives off their ancestral land in the Southeastern United States to areas west of the Mississippi River in modern day Oklahoma.

It was a 1,200-mile journey and around 4,000 Natives died along the way. It is estimated between 1831 and 1877, around 60,000 Natives were driven from their homeland.

The locations they were forced to inhabit were not the best of the land and held little opportunity for them to live independently and flourish into the thriving nation the Natives once enjoyed. Here is how then President Andrew Jackson justified the cruel law:

Jackson's involvement in what became known as the Trail of Tears cannot be ignored. In a speech regarding Indian removal, Jackson said, "It will separate the Indians from immediate contact with settlements of whites; free them from the power of the States; enable them to pursue happiness in their own way and under their own rude institutions; will retard the progress of decay, which is lessening their numbers, and perhaps cause them gradually, under the protection of the Government and through the influence of good counsels, to cast off their savage habits and become an interesting, civilized, and Christian community. (Wikipedia - Trail of Tears)

In Jackson's remarks, the first goal mentioned in the Indian Removal Act was the separation between white settlers and the Natives. Separation is always the goal of systemic racism.

Today, some crumbling inner cities with few high-quality job opportunities, stumbling education systems, and little to no access to quality healthcare, are recipes for failure that affect present and future generations in the areas of economics, social interaction, and education.

However, these systemic racism situations are not insurmountable or the sole cause that many blacks remain behind the equality curve. Numerous blacks, despite these barriers, have overcome and made tremendous economic strides, proving systemic racism, when faced with determination, proper assistance, and re-sources, cannot stop a person's progress to financial, educational, and health success.

✳✳✳

Church: The Refuge for Racism

Throughout American history racism has found safe refuge in several major societal institutions such as religion, politics, law enforcement, education, and financial institutions. A refuge can be defined as a place of safety where a person or thing can be protected and given all the necessities of life. As a result, the refugee can feel safe and comfortable.

For supremacy and racism to survive several centuries, they must have a place of refuge and people willing to teach, believe, and disseminate them to others. The seven major institutions of America had to be painfully and slowly integrated—at times with the cost of human life.

Church: Blacks were denied access to some white churches and split from others because some white leaders did not allow them to worship or pray in the same area as whites—suggesting blacks were inferior. Many of those splits continue today.

Education: Blacks were denied access to quality education and had to fight to integrate white school systems. In 1960 and at the tender age of six, Ruby Bridges became the first black girl to integrate an elementary school in the south. She was escorted to class by U.S. marshals and her mother due to violent mobs.

Law Enforcement: The police force in the south, pre-civil and post-civil war, was predominantly white and remains so in many areas today. Minorities who integrated often faced stiff racism. The first black police officer hired in Birmingham Alabama was Jessie Mack in 1974.

Politics: Blacks faced multiple layers of opposition to political power ranging from voter suppression, denial to ballot access, and threats from those who opposed black representation. In 1870, just five years after the civil war, the first black congressman, Hiram Rhodes Revels, took his oath of office, but not without opposition from southern whites who did not want black representatives.

Military: African soldiers who volunteered to fight for the Union Army during the civil war were not treated as equals. They were placed in "colored" regiments instead of serving side by side with whites. In 1948 President Truman signed an executive order mandating equality of treatment and opportunity in the military.

Economic: Racist lending practices such as denial of lending and high interest rates became the norm in the post-civil war south and persisted despite attempts by the federal government to insure lending equality.

Social: Southern state laws such as "pig" laws, black codes, and Jim Crow laws were instituted to maintain racial separation in society. Integration in dining, shopping, and other social activities were highly discouraged. Blacks used store sit ins to protest.

I want to share specifically about the institution of religion—particularly the Christian church. For over 400 years, these discriminatory beliefs and practices have found refuge in the powerful and influential American church.

Clearly, all white Christians are not supremacists or racists. In fact, many support racial equality and perform their spiritual practices with the utmost compassion for all people. But there are some leaders and parishioners who have willingly adopted the teachings and practices of white supremacy and racism. Those people tend to feel safe believing and practicing discrimination simply because, like in a refuge, they will not be called out, challenged, nor disciplined for the sinful acts of racism.

It will help to examine it from a historical perspective till today. Before the civil war, English settlers had occupied the Southern states and had accumulated massive wealth by providing raw materials in the trade triangle with European nations. Southern states specialized in growing cash crops such as tobacco, rice, and cotton. But these crops required a large amount of physical labor to be profitable.

The settlers began by using hired labor from European countries. These people were usually poor whites looking to improve their life. They entered into contracts and agreements to labor for pay. When the contracts were completed, these white laborers usually went back to Europe or stayed and moved further inland to establish their own places to live. Thus, employers had issues keeping labor.

They began to use African slaves as laborers and that was a far better solution than paid white laborers who had short terms of employment. As international trade grew and more land was taken from the Natives, the need for black slaves to work the land also grew.

These English settlers were mostly Christian Protestants who came to America to live, work the land, and make money. An online article entitled How Slavery Became the Economic Engine of the South, Greg Timmons, Dec 2019, states:

> *Slavery was so profitable, it sprouted more millionaires per capita in the Mississippi River Valley than anywhere in the nation.*

With such massive wealth came power, prestige, and comfortable lifestyles that eventually had to be justified to Northern Abolitionists who found southern slavery to be repugnant and immoral. Also, the cheap slave labor of the south became competitive with northern whites seeking to provide labor for new territories that were opened. Thus, slavery had become an economic problem as well as a moral issue.

Some southern church leaders had to develop a moral argument for forced slavery, a justification for white supremacy and racism, and a moral response to arguments from Abolitionists.

Some pastors and parishioners used the institution of religion and perverted biblical scriptures, took others completely out of context, and ignored the scriptures that required them to treat blacks with love and compassion. The church soon became permeated with pastors and clergy who taught not only the acceptance of slavery, but the supposed divine supremacy of the white race.

James Henley Thornwell, a pre-civil war southern pastor, regularly defended slavery and promoted white supremacy from his pulpit at the First Presbyterian Church in Columbia, South Carolina. Using the teachings of Paul and Peter, which both instruct slaves to obey their masters, he indoctrinated churchgoers with the false sense of human bondage justification and racial superiority.

But those false teachings did not die with his generation. Instead, they passed from one church to another, from one family to another, and from one generation to another. A preacher named William Joseph Simmons used the Christian faith to revive the Klu Klux Klan on stone mountain Georgia in 1915. Some churchgoers in Montgomery Alabama used their children to help attack civil rights protestors during a freedom bus ride in May 1961.

Today, in 2020, supremacy and racism in some white congregations is still alive and well protected, nourished, and continuously passed to new generations by false proclamation, apathy, and indifference to the continued struggles of blacks and other minorities.

As proof of this, a survey was done that suggested racism may be higher among church going Christians than among nonreligious people. Below, is a portion of the online article entitled Racism Among White Christians is Higher than Among Nonreligious. That's no coincidence. July 2020:

> *White Christians are consistently more likely than whites who are religiously unaffiliated to deny the existence of structural racism.*

How could it be, after over 400 years, that racism continues to be taught and learned in the place where it should not exist at all—the Christian church? An online article entitled White Christian America Needs a Moral Awakening, July 2020, summed up the moral issue:

White Christian churches have not just been complacent or complicit in failing to address racism; rather, as the dominant cultural power in the U.S., they have been responsible for constructing and sustaining a project to protect white supremacy.

Rosa, a Hispanic friend, shared a stunning story about racism that she encountered in the 1980s. She was a young military mother with two young children. After locating to Pennsylvania, she enlisted the help of a real estate agent to find a home. She chose a house in an all-white neighborhood.

A few days later, someone broke the windows out of her home. Terrified for the safety of her children, she moved to another state.

Through a news article about the event, she later learned the thoughts and comments about the racist attack from some neighbors, including a clergyman who seemed to blame the real estate agent for selling the house to a minority.

She was surprised that the clergyman did not support her and try to intervene. I suppose most of us expect those who represent God to do the godly thing and stand up for those who are being abused and attacked. But that will never happen if some white clergy and congregants continue to submit to their fears and give refuge to the immoral sins of supremacy and racism.

White fear is real. All races have their respective fears, but the specific fears that fuel and elicit racist acts in some whites are particularly potent.

There is the fear of losing power and ending up subject to minority leaders. This can lead to extensive voter suppression tactics.

There is the fear of losing wealth and income—possibly becoming one of the little people. This can lead to unfair lending practices.

There is the fear of the loss of safety and succumbing to violent savages or low-lives of society. This can lead to inequality in law enforcement and justice system.

Historically, these fears have been stoked and stirred by supremacists, racists, and political figures, and have led to some of America's deadliest attacks such as the 1921 Tulsa, Oklahoma attacks.

Here is a fitting end from the same article about racism presenting itself more often among Christians than Among Nonreligious:

> *As monuments to white supremacy are falling all across America, a great cloud of witnesses is gathering. Our fellow African American citizens, and indeed the entire country, are waiting to see whether we white Christians can finally find the humility and courage and love to face the truth about our long relationship with white supremacy and to dismantle the Christian worldview we built to justify it.*

The discouraging truth is the One-Race (all humans are one race) truth of the Christian faith continues to be minimized, ignored, and even rejected by many in the very institution charged with promoting it: The Christian Church.

If you are a white Christian leader, have you taught on the sin of racism? If you are a black Christian leader, have you taught on the sin of racism and forgiveness for past slavery and current racism?

I still believe the Christian church is the most spiritually powerful organism on the face of the earth. And I continue to have confidence in Christian leaders in America and around the world that they will eventually unite, confront the surge of racism, and demonstrate the true love of Jesus Christ. The time is now.

Two: Self-Evaluation & Discussion

Do you believe systemic racism still exists? Why or Why not?

Have you experienced what you believe to be systemic racism? Please share with the group if you can.

In your opinion, what things can be done to identify and combat systemic racism?

What other points would you want to group-discuss in this chapter?

CHAPTER THREE

THE BIBLE and RACISM

I met Jim in 2008. He was a Caucasian Christian with whom I had opposing political views. We became good friends despite our differences in political philosophies.

One day our deep conversation veered into the realm of racism. I thought we had little in common on the subject. However, I was surprised by his testimony.

"Charlie," he said as he looked intently at me. "There was a time when I harbored deep racist opinions and thoughts."

I was startled and struggled to push out words.

"You?" I finally managed to whisper. "But we've always gotten along just fine. In fact, we've talked about some intensely personal subjects at times. I can't imagine you being a racist."

He smiled and continued. "I believe the word is ex-racist. Everyone who truly belongs to Jesus is an ex-something."

My face formed a confused frown. "But you've been a Christian for a long time. How could you have been a racist and love Jesus the way you do?"

He thought for a moment and began to explain. "I was taught, even by some church members, that certain verses in the Bible justified racism."

I gasped in disbelief. He began sharing those scriptures that were misused as I sat in total amazement—taking in the verses that were clearly misinterpreted.

"But those verses don't justify racism," I interrupted.

"I know they don't," he replied. "I suppose I always knew they didn't. Now that I've truly met Jesus and grown to love Him with all my heart, somehow, I just can't continue living with those evil thoughts and ways. He changed my whole life. He has a way of doing that, you know."

I noticed the tears welling up in his eyes and his countenance of complete peace. I gently put my hand on his shoulder and softly responded, "I know."

I believe life is like driving an automobile that has three types of mirrors. There is the sideview mirror that is designed to look at cars along each side of the vehicle. There is the rearview mirror used to observe cars coming from the rear. There is the self-view mirror, usually found in the sun visor, used to view yourself and make any needed corrections.

The sideview and rearview mirrors are used most often. In other words, some people can spend most of their time judging, condemning, and correcting others—but never taking the necessary time to examine themselves.

My white brother understood he couldn't change the people in his church or some of the people in his family—but he could change himself. I learned a valuable lesson from his testimony. If I want other people to change, I can't force that change upon them. I must first demonstrate the very change I'm looking for in them.

If I want a person to be respectful, I must first respect that individual. If I want a person to treat me as equal, I must first treat that person as equal. If I want a person to love me, I must first love that person. As I demonstrate these things other people, I must also allow them a choice: to return my actions or to reject them.

I'm convinced race relations won't improve by seeking out racists and making them pay in one way or the other. They will improve only when all people, regardless of their race, spend significant time gazing into the self-view mirror of their own thoughts and opinions.

After our soul-searching conversation, I couldn't help but look deeply into the self-view mirror of my own thoughts and opinions—determining not to harbor or tolerate racist beliefs, teachings, and actions in myself nor the ones I love.

$$* * *$$

The Bible & Racism

The following quote comes from an online article entitled, White Supremacist Ideas Have Historical Roots in U.S. Christianity.

> *"Less than three weeks after the 1961 attack on the Freedom Riders, Montgomery's most prominent pastor, Henry Lyon, Jr., gave a fiery speech before the local white Citizens' Council denouncing the civil rights protesters and the cause for which they were beaten — from a "Christian" perspective.*

> *"Ladies and gentlemen, for 15 years I have had the priv-*
> *ilege of being pastor of a white Baptist church in this*
> *city," Lyon said. "If we stand 100 years from now, it will*
> *still be a white church. I am a believer in a separation of*
> *the races, and I am none the less a Christian." The crowd*
> *applauded."*

The Holy Bible has been used for centuries in unholy ways by three groups of people. The first group is comprised of those who are pure evil. The second group refers to those who misunderstand and misinterpret the Word of God. And the third includes those who are deceptive, and for personal reasons, choose to ignore certain scriptures that do not aid their cause or prove their point of view.

Supremacists and racists are in all three categories. Some are pure evil and pervert certain scriptures to advance the sin of white supremacy. Some are ignorant of the truth and misinterpret verses they do not understand—applying them in a racist way.

Others know right from wrong because of their conscience and knowledge of the Bible. However, they willingly ignore the scriptures that clearly state the truth about the evils of racism and choose to highlight and promote sections of the Word of God that seem to justify racism.

Here is what Pastor Henry Lyons, Jr. said according to the article:

> *"If you want to get in a fight with the one that started*
> *separation of the races, then you come face to face with*
> *your God," he declared. "The difference in color, the dif-*
> *ference in our body, our minds, our life, our mission*
> *upon the face of this earth, is God given."*

The powerful position of pastoring, especially in the south, has always been a highly influential occupation. People respect the preacher and tend to give the person occupying that spiritual position credibility and the benefit of the doubt. They tend to do so even when they do not fully understand or agree with the message. The preaching of white supremacy, racism, and racial separation as permissible or even as God's will, was integral to the wide acceptance of slavery by many church goers in the south.

They used the distorted Christian message of the black curse and white purity to silence their consciences and to disconnect emotionally, mentally, and psychologically from the misery, pain, and suffering inflicted upon African slaves.

During slavery times, some preachers had personal reasons for declaring blacks to be cursed and doomed. Some were deeply invested in the highly profitable business of slavery. The same article quotes a preacher's 1861 sermon in favor of slavery. He was a slave owner and pastor named Thornwell who declared Christians should not feel guilty about owning slaves. Here are portions of his fiery messages.

> "The relation of master and slave stands on the same foot with the other relations of life," Thornwell insisted. " In itself, it is not inconsistent with the will of God. It is not sinful."
>
> "The Christian Scriptures," Thornwell said, "not only fail to condemn; they as distinctly sanction slavery as any other social condition of man."

One of Thornwell's favorite scriptures used to support slavery was:

"Slaves, obey your earthly masters with respect and fear, and with sincerity of heart, just as you would obey Christ."

(Ephesians 6:5 ESV)

At that time, Thornwell pastored a church that contained slave owners, businessmen, and other members of the social elite. Therefore, it was financially beneficial to preach the acceptance of slavery. He used the Christian pulpit and the Holy Bible to defend the south from accusations of northern abolitionists claims that slavery was immoral and unjust.

But what does the Bible really say about supremacy, racism, and discrimination? Did the God of the Christian faith allow slavery, and if so, why? Are Africans cursed and doomed to be lower-level society servants? Did God create different races or did humans? Is any race superior? Does God oppose interracial relationships and blended families? These questions will be answered in the following sections.

Question:
What does the Bible teach about supremacy, racism, and discrimination?

Answer:
The Holy Bible condemns all three. They are sin in the eyes of God.

Supremacy is the exalting of oneself above others and attributing more value to oneself than intended by God. It is based on ungodly pride which is one of the four pillars of racism shared in a previous chapter. It takes ungodly pride and arrogance to claim a high level of self-importance that God did not grant. Supremacy claims: "I am first and of utmost importance in the eyes of God; others exist merely to serve me."

Here are a few Biblical scriptures about humility:

> *"The greatest among you shall be your servant. Whoever exalts himself will be humbled, and whoever humbles himself will be exalted. "* *(Matthew 23:11-12 ESV)*
>
> *"Do nothing from rivalry or conceit, but in humility count others more significant than yourselves."* *(Philippians 2:3 ESV)*
>
> *"For by the grace given to me I say to everyone among you not to think of himself more highly than he ought to think, but to think with sober judgment, each according to the measure of faith that God has assigned."* *(Romans 12:3 ESV)*

The supremacy mindset is contrary to the Christian faith and against every teaching of Jesus Christ and other biblical writers. Pride considers itself more important than others while humility considers others more important than self. Pride seeks others to serve itself, while humility seeks to serve others. People infected with spiritual pride will often use the Holy Scriptures to justify or emphasize what others should do for them.

In the chapter opening, the Pastor used a scripture telling slaves to obey their masters. In other words, his message was,

"You black slaves, serve your masters like the Bible tells you to do."

Supremacy is arrogance at its finest. It is based on a lie that God made one race more important than another. It is based on the selfishness and greed of wanting wealth, power, and elevated social status that is undeserving. Supremacy, which is an expression of pride (haughtiness), is demonically influenced, highly immoral, and one of the seven deadly sins God hates.

"There are six things that the LORD hates,

seven that are an abomination to him:

17 haughty eyes, a lying tongue,

and hands that shed innocent blood,

18 a heart that devises wicked plans,

feet that make haste to run to evil,

19 a false witness who breathes out lies,

and one who sows discord among brothers."

(Proverbs 6:16-19 ESV)

Jesus Christ taught humility as one of his hallmark lessons. At times, Jesus became frustrated with his disciples because of their constant tendency to elevate their self-importance.

At one point, two of them secretly cornered Jesus and asked him to allow one to sit on His left and another on His right when Jesus came into His kingdom. They wanted positions of notoriety and power. On another occasion, they argued among themselves as to who was the greatest in Heaven. Their minds were in the wrong place.

Jesus had to demonstrate true humility by washing their feet. They were shocked and dismayed when Jesus pulled off his outer clothing, tied a towel around his waist, and as any common slave did in his day, washed their feet (John 13:1-17).

Supremacists and leaders in the southern states had the same problem as Jesus' disciples. They wanted positions of prominence and notoriety at the expense of African slaves. Supremacy was a foundational teaching of the south because it gave some antebellum whites wealth, status, and privilege. Justifying slavery by misusing the scriptures was just one method they used to keep the status quo.

Pride leads to supremacy (exalting oneself), supremacy leads to racism (unjust separation), and racism leads to discrimination (unfair acts against others). They are all related and when practiced, result in human misery and the fiery judgement of God.

Other texts on Pride (Pro 8:13, 16:18, Rom 12:16, 2 Cor 10:17-18)

Question: Did God allow slavery and were blacks destined to be slaves?

Answer: Yes, He did. And no, blacks were not destined to be slaves.

Thornwell's claim that slavery was not forbidden in the Bible was correct. But his claim that slavery was the destiny of blacks was not correct. He said:

"As long as that [African] race, in its comparative degradation, co-exists side by side with the white," Thornwell declared in a famous 1861 sermon, "bondage is its normal condition."

Throughout history and in Biblical times, slavery was commonplace and widely accepted. In His permissive will, God allowed it to exist even among His chosen people Israel (Exodus 12:44-48).

There were two main ways a person could become a slave. One way was by the involuntary means of capture in a war, kidnapping, or pirating. The second way was by voluntary means of selling oneself or a relative due to extreme poverty, default on a debt, or loss in gambling to name a few.

Though God allowed these slavery situations to occur, there is proof in the Bible that He did not want people to be slaves for their entire lives. He gave his servant Moses a law referred to by scholars as The Year of Jubilee—a time when all slaves were to be set free. It occurred every fifty-years and included the freedom of slaves, wiping out of any debt owed, and the return of any land that had been confiscated to pay a debt (Leviticus 25).

This freedom is called manumission and served as proof that God did not want people permanently enslaved, indebted, nor sinking in poverty because of the loss of their land. Thus, God's perfect will for humans is to be free and capable of providing for themselves.

The New Testament letters of Paul and Peter (Ephesians 6:5-8, Colossians 3:22-25, Philemon, and 1 Peter 2:18-21) were often referenced by pro-slave pastors to justify the bondage of blacks. But most Bible scholars agree the type of slavery Paul and Peter referred to is legal slavery or situations of voluntary slavery where persons either sold themselves or were legally sold.

Thus, when Paul advises slaves to get their freedom if possible, he was saying to do so by legal means such as paying for their freedom or by some other method. (1 Corinthians 7:17-24)

Voluntary bond-servant relationships were legally binding in many societies and governed by legal authorities.

However, involuntary slavery such as kidnapping and illegally selling someone without having the authority to do so was frowned upon and the Apostle Paul even listed it among other sins--referring to people who did such things as menstealers in King James Version. Interpreted as slave-traders in some other versions of the Bible.

> *"Knowing this, that the law is not made for a righteous man, but for the lawless and disobedient, for the ungodly and for sinners, for unholy and profane, for murderers of fathers and murderers of mothers, for manslayers, For whoremongers, for them that defile themselves with mankind, for menstealers, for liars, for perjured persons, and if there be any other thing that is contrary to sound doctrine;" (1 Timothy 1:9-10 KJV)*

The African slave trade was not a voluntary slave arrangement entered into for a specific period or until a debt was paid. It was an illegal, lifelong slave-trade operation. African tribal leaders kidnapped and pirated their own race and collaborated with white European slave traders who bought blacks and shipped them to multiple continents across the Atlantic Ocean—all against their will.

That is the type of slavery Paul condemned in the Bible and why northern slave abolitionists constantly sparred with southern slave owners. Northerners declared the forced black-market slave trading, along with southerners' ill-treatment of blacks, to be immoral and unjust.

But some southern pastors and leaders continued to use perverted Bible verses to justify their sin and to amass wealth, power, and prestige—all while claiming to be God-fearing Christians.

In an online article for Time magazine referencing slave history entitled, How Christian Slaveholders used the Bible to Justify Slavery, February 2018, the author writes about Fredrick Douglas, a black former slave who legally gained his freedom.

He was an Abolitionist and friend of President Abraham Lincoln who made this stunning comparison of real Christianity to the professed Christianity of some white congregations that supported slavery.

"Between the Christianity of this land and the Christianity of Christ, I recognize the widest possible difference—so wide that to receive the one as good, pure, and holy, is of necessity to reject the other as bad, corrupt, and wicked. To be the friend of the one is of necessity to be the enemy of the other.

I love the pure, peaceable, and impartial Christianity of Christ; I therefore hate the corrupt, slave-holding, women-whipping, cradle-plundering, partial and hypocritical Christianity of this land. Indeed, I can see no reason but the most deceitful one for calling the religion of this land Christianity..."

In a previous section, I challenged those white congregations who continue to embrace racism to go beyond having the form of Christianity and live out the totality of the faith. That includes denouncing white supremacy within the congregation, acknowledging that racism still exists and is systemic, and fighting against racism by standing up for equal justice and equality. That is what the God of the Christian faith wants from all His children no matter their skin color.

Question:
Was the black race cursed and is the white race superior?

Answer:
No and No. The black race was not cursed, and God did not make any race superior.

The occurrence of the 1994 Genocide in Rwanda Africa is a reminder of how dangerous it is to claim racial superiority by misinterpreting Bible scriptures. The African Hutu tribe attacked the Tutsi tribe, and when the killing ended, around 800,000 Tutsi and moderate Hutus were murdered—hacked by machetes, dismembered, and slaughtered in other ways.

Although the conflict had several complex causes, one of the main drivers was the hatred the Hutus developed for their Tutsi brothers and sisters. They always had their differences, but that was magnified when European colonists brought the concept of race to the African Tribes.

An online article explains how European colonists used the famous story of "The curse of Ham" in the Bible to assign superiority to the Tutsi tribe and inferiority to the Hutu tribe.

After years of racism and discrimination against the Hutus, they finally had enough. That is when the killing began.

Here is the misinterpreted Bible story European colonists used which is the same one recited by Southern pastors and slave owners to teach the curse of the black race and justify African slavery leading up to the civil war.

> *"The sons of Noah who went forth from the ark were Shem, Ham, and Japheth. (Ham was the father of Canaan.) 19 These three were the sons of Noah, and from these the people of the whole earth were dispersed.*
>
> *Noah began to be a man of the soil, and he planted a vineyard. He drank of the wine and became drunk and lay uncovered in his tent. And Ham, the father of Canaan, saw the nakedness of his father and told his two brothers outside. Then Shem and Japheth took a garment, laid it on both their shoulders, and walked backward and covered the nakedness of their father. Their faces were turned backward, and they did not see their father's nakedness.*
>
> *When Noah awoke from his wine hand knew what his youngest son had done to him, he said, "Cursed be Canaan; a servant of servants shall he be to his brothers." He also said, "Blessed be the LORD, the God of Shem;*
>
> *and let Canaan be his servant.*
>
> *May God enlarge Japheth,*
>
> *and let him dwell in the tents of Shem,*
>
> *and let Canaan be his servant."*
>
> *(Genesis 9:18-27 ESV)*

According to the biblical account, Noah had three sons—Shem, Ham, and Japheth. Noah's sons have been divided by historians into three races. Shem was assigned to the Semitic race (Jewish, etc), Japheth to the European race (Caucasians), and Ham to the African race (Black).

As the scriptures explain, Ham disrespected his father Noah in some way that is not fully understood. As a result, Noah did not curse Ham (Ham had been previously blessed by God), but cursed Canaan who was Ham's fourth son. Noah proclaimed that Canaan (and his descendants) would be slaves to the descendants of Shem (Jewish, etc) and Japheth (Caucasian, etc).

First, the exact time of this occurrence cannot be known, but we can say it happened well over 4,000 years ago. That fact alone should pose the question: Has anything changed from then till now, and does this curse still apply today?

Yes, much has changed, and the curse does not apply today nor did it apply during pre-civil war. Many scholars agree the curse was fulfilled in history—long before the 17th century slave trade and the 1994 Rwanda genocide.

Second, Ham represented the entire black race. Ham was not cursed, but his fourth son, Canaan. That means Ham's three other sons, Cush, Egypt (Mizraim), and Put, also members of the black race—were not cursed (1 Chronicles 2:8).

And third, Jesus Christ received power over all curses when He died on the cross and rose from the dead (Colossians 2:6-15). God did not want any race, including Canaan's descendants, to be doomed forever under a curse—so He sent His only Son, in the likeness of humans, to die for the sins of the world and remove all curses. The Bible says He became a curse for us so that we would not have to endure curses.

> *"13 Christ redeemed us from the curse of the law by becoming a curse for us—for it is written, "Cursed is everyone who is hanged on a tree"— 14 so that in Christ Jesus the blessing of Abraham might come to the Gentiles, so that we might receive the promised Spirit through faith."*
>
> *(Galatians 3:13-14 ESV)*

Jesus took all the curses we deserved, whether inflicted by us or our ancestors, and nailed them to His cross when He was crucified. That includes the curse of Ham's son Canaan. No longer does any descendent of Canaan have to live with a 4,000-year-old curse. The blood of Jesus Christ killed the curse!

Here is how one person explained Christ becoming a curse for us in an online article by Igniting Hope entitled What Does it Mean That Jesus Became a Curse for Us? August 2016:

Jesus took all the curses that I deserved because of the choices made by my ancestors and me. He offers to me a great exchange. Therefore, some southern pastors and Christians should not have used the curse of Ham as an excuse to enslave blacks.

White Purity

The Bible often uses the color white or the word light as a metaphor to represent purity and righteousness, while using the color black or the word dark as a metaphor for sin or bad occurrences.

> *"After this I looked, and behold, a great multitude that no one could number, from every nation, from all tribes and peoples and languages, standing before the throne and before the Lamb, clothed in white robes, with palm branches in their hands, and crying out with a loud voice, "Salvation belongs to our God who sits on the throne, and to the Lamb!"*
>
> *(Revelation 7:9-10 ESV)*
>
> *"Rise, shine, for your light has come, and the glory of the LORD has risen upon you. For behold, darkness shall cover the earth, and thick darkness the peoples; but the LORD will arise upon you, and his glory will be seen upon you. And nations shall come to your light, and kings to the brightness of your rising." (Isaiah 60:1-3 ESV)*

These Biblical references are metaphoric only and only a figure of speech used as a comparison and should not be interpreted to literally mean white and black people. Supremacists and racists tend to misuse these passages by equating white metaphors to mean the white race and black metaphors to mean the black race. This is the basis of their false claim that white people are pure and good, while black people are cursed and bad.

Notice, in the previous scriptures, Revelation 7:9-10, people from all races (nations, tribes, people, languages) were standing before the throne and ALL people had on white robes—not just the white race.

The Christian faith clearly defines what makes a person pure in the eyes of God, and that is not the color of a person's skin but the condition of a person's heart (the center of spiritual activity and all human life).

> *"Blessed are the pure in heart, for they shall see God."*
>
> *(Matthew 5:18 ESV)*

> *"Who shall ascend the hill of the LORD?*
>
> *And who shall stand in his holy place?*
>
> *He who has clean hands and a pure heart..."*
>
> *(Psalms 24:3-4)*

Jesus communicated this truth to the people of Israel in several ways because some of them thought the Jewish race was pure and superior to other races.

> *"And he said, "What comes out of a person is what de-files him. For from within, out of the heart of man, come evil thoughts, sexual immorality, theft, murder, adultery, coveting, wickedness, deceit, sensuality, envy, slander, pride, foolishness. All these evil things come from within, and they defile a person."*
>
> *(Mark 7:20-23 ESV)*

The Apostle Peter said it best, that ignorant people tend to pervert and distort the Holy Scriptures for their own personal gain.

> *"Therefore, beloved, since you are waiting for these, be diligent to be found by him without spot or blemish, and at peace. And count the patience of our Lord as salvation, just as our beloved brother Paul also wrote to you according to the wisdom given him, as he does in all his letters when he speaks in them of these matters. There are some things in them that are hard to understand,*

> *which the ignorant and unstable twist to their own destruction, as they do the other Scriptures.*

> *You therefore, beloved, knowing this beforehand, take care that you are not carried away with the error of lawless people and lose your own stability. But grow in the grace and knowledge of our Lord and Savior Jesus Christ. To him be the glory both now and to the day of eternity. Amen."*
>
> *(2 Peter 3:14-18 ESV)*

Peter's warning in the previous scripture applies today. We should be careful when dealing with lawless people who misuse the Bible for their own evil purpose.

Here is a summation of what happened in Rwanda when the story of Ham's curse was taken out of context. Taken from an online article entitled The Curse of Ham: How Bad Scripture Interpretation Inspired Genocide by Eliza Thomas, June 2018:

> *Along with their philosophy of history, Europeans brought to Africa the idea of race . . . Hutu and Tutsi existed in precolonial Rwanda as roles that determined people's place in society.*

> *But Europeans ascribed biblical explanations to these roles, insisting that they could see in Tutsis' physical features that they were descendants of Semites. The same 'science' that was used to justify slavery also measured nose width and calculated average height in order to demonstrate Tutsi superiority.*

The story of the curse of Ham was not only abused in Rwanda Africa to turn blacks against each other, it was also misused in America, pre-Civil War, by some Southern Christians to create the tribalism of white supremacy and black inferiority.

It is a shame that those who touted their fear of God and patriotism, did not recognize the power of the blood of Christ nor the love of God toward all races.

It appears that white supremacists, instead of humbling themselves after claiming Christianity, allowed greed and the blood of tribalism to flow deeper than the waters of baptism—which washes away all boasting and pride of the flesh and makes a new creation. The Bible says,

> "Therefore, if anyone is in Christ, he is a new creation. The old has passed away; behold, the new has come."
>
> (2 Corinthians 5:17 ESV)

Question:
Does the Bible forbid interracial relationships and blended families?

Answer:
No. God and Jesus Christ both validated mixed marriages and blended families.

White supremacists and racists both detest interracial relationships such as racially mixed marriages and blended families. They wrongfully claim that their pure white blood should not be tainted with the blood of other races. They have a history of rejecting, harassing, and even attacking mixed couples and

blended families. Like the curse of Ham story, they misinterpret other biblical scriptures to prove their twisted view of
God's word.

God made humans. Humans divided themselves into races
based on their ancestors, places they lived, and physical appearances. According to the lineage of the Bible itself, all humans
on earth today are descendants of Noah and his wife, and eventually traced back to Adam and Eve, the first humans God
created.

Therefore, it is not possible for any race to have a pure
bloodline that is superior to others if we all came from the same
man and woman: (Genesis 5:1-32).

Second, at times, God did forbid ancient Israel from marry-
ing into certain nations (sometimes interpreted as races). But
the reason was spiritual, not racial. God did not want Israel to
be led astray by the idol worship of other nations (Deuteronomy
7:1-3).

Third, God approved of the interracial marriage of Moses
(Semitic Hebrew) to a Cushite (Black Ethiopian) woman.
When Moses' marriage came under attack by his brother Aaron
and sister Miriam, God punished Miriam by inflicting her with
leprosy. She was quarantined for a period before returning to
her people. (Numbers 12:1-16).

And fourth, Jesus spoke well of the Samaritans—a mixed
race of people whom some Jews hated so much that they trav-
eled for miles around the Samaritan city just to avoid contact
with them. Jesus witnessed to a Samaritan woman, stayed in
their town for days, and even made a Samaritan man the hero
of one of his stories (Luke 10:25-37).

A long history of racism in America and in other parts of the world has led many people to believe there is something immoral about interracial relationships. It has also caused some children to feel ashamed or even unworthy at times.

The United States Supreme Court struck down anti-miscegenation laws which banned interracial marriages. All those laws were declared unconstitutional by the U. S. Supreme Court in 1967.

The beauty about the Christian faith is the spiritual disappearance of tribal lines and other things that divide us and cause us to fight against each other. We should not judge ourselves or others according to these tribal lines. In Jesus, we gain a new and more powerful identity that is spiritual—we are sons and daughters of God. The apostle Paul stated the equality of all people without regard to racial/ethnic background and social status.

> *"You are all sons of God through faith in Christ Jesus, for all of you who were baptized into Christ have clothed yourselves with Christ. There is neither Jew nor Greek, slave nor free, male nor female, for you are all one in Christ Jesus."*
>
> *(Galatians 3:26-28 ESV)*

It is beautiful when we allow the pure and perfect blood of Jesus Christ to wash away our fleshy tribal lines.

How to Talk to Youths About Race

As parents, teachers, and Christian leaders, we all have a very difficult task in explaining racial subject matter to youths. I never envisioned this book becoming a common tool for adults and youths to share, but it became just that. After having a race workshop for one church, days later, the Pastor called and said to me, "I had one father who read and discussed the book with his young children. Hours later, they were still reading and talking."

How do we share tidbits of truth, wisdom, and advice on such a contentious subject as race? Here are some suggestions.

One, give youths a godly view of colors, shapes, and sizes. Help them to realized why God used so much color in everything He created. Take a walk-through Genesis chapter one where God created something special on each of the six days and used color in a B.I.G. way. God used colors, shapes, and sizes to Beautify, Identify, and Glorify.

Beautify: to make things look pleasant and attractive. God wanted humans to have a good experience when we look at things and people of different colors. (Genesis 1, 2:9, Revelations 21)

Identify: to give everything in creation a unique identity. There is no one like God, and He only wanted one person just like you! Your color, shape, and size are all part of your unique identity. (Psalms 139:13-14)

Glorify: to make humans think about God and His creative ability. God wanted humans to see His handiwork in all of creation from trees and flowers, sea creatures and land animals, to human beings. He wanted us to exclaim, "Wow! Look at what God has done!" (Genesis 1:1, Psalms 19:1, Job 12:7-10)

Two, help them see God created color, not races. God did not create races. Over time, people took the beautiful colors, shapes, and sizes of humans, and created categories called races. And in their sinful ways, they placed people into groups with dividing lines for the express purpose of gaining some advantage. They invented racism and racial injustice which God hates. (Genesis 6:5-6, Exodus 1:8-14)

Three, help them see God does not separate or discriminate. God does not use people's color, shape, or size to separate or segregate them into groups nor to keep people from integrating (becoming a part of or joined with) people of different races. God judges a person based upon his or her heart, not race.
(1 Samuel 16:7, Revelation 7:9-10)

Four, teach them how to set the example and how to respond to racism. It is hard today in this world of pressure for youths to set the example. But you can encourage them to do so by instructing them to:

Not join in when others make racist jokes.

Not participate when someone is being racially bullied.

Befriend people of different races at school by asking them questions about their customs and cultures.

Speak up in a non-confrontational way when they witness racism against others.

Keep calm and walk away when someone verbally attacks them. (Matthew 22:37-39, 1Timothy 4:12, 3 John 11)

Ask youths open-ended questions with the aim of getting them to share their feelings, thoughts, and experiences. Questions such as:

Why do you think racism hurts God?

Tell me about a friend or person you know of another race.

Tell me about your racial experience at school.

If you choose to walk through God's creation in Genesis chapter one, pause and talk about each day of creation. Use imagery and describe your favorite colors or share a wonderful experience you had related to that creation. Ask youths to describe their favorite experiences and invite them to talk about why they loved or admired certain colors, shapes, and sizes in nature. Then establish a connection with nature and humans. Help them apply the same admiration they have for nature to humans.

Keep the communication channel open. It is not enough to talk about one time and never mention it again. Youths are always faced with extreme challenges and pressure to do the wrong things. You and I need to always be there to talk, listen, and encourage them not to fall in line with others, but to stand out by standing up for what is right.

Three: Self-Evaluation & Discussion

Have you heard the claim that black people were either cursed or lowest on the race chain?

If you are a person of faith, have you witnessed faith writings being used to promote or justify racism?

What are some negative racial perceptions you once believed but have changed your mind about?

What other points would you want to group-discuss in this chapter?

CHAPTER FOUR

WHITE and BLACK CHALLENGES

In 2005 I was sitting in my parked car in a church parking lot. I slowly inhaled and exhaled. I prayed for a long time to see this day. Finally, my prayers were answered. A door of opportunity to speak at a white congregation finally opened. I sat motionless outside the little church in Tennessee, quietly reflecting on the words I was about to share with my Caucasian brothers and sisters.

"I wonder what they are expecting from a black preacher?" I pondered. "I hope they don't expect me to break out with a line of old Negro spirituals or hound them with the evils of racism."

I chuckled, exited the car, and encountered several people as I approached the entrance.

"Good morning," one person offered. I kindly returned her greeting with a soft tone and a smile. Then it happened again, and again, and again. Several people greeted me with warmth, compassion, and love. I thought, these people are really Christians.

I found the person who invited me, and we walked through the church, meeting people as we went. We stopped at their nursery where a middle-aged woman sat in a rocking chair, surrounded by several infants and a teenaged girl.

"This is Minister Holley," my host announced. "He is our speaker for today."

The teenager flashed a smile and continued playing with the infants. The woman glanced at me, smiled, and began to recite words from one of my previous messages—word for word.

Surprised, I managed to ask, "You've heard me speak?"

"A friend of mine gave me a disc with one of your sermons," she replied. "I played it so much that I wore out the disc."

We laughed.

"That's good to know," I replied. We made our way back inside the sanctuary where the service began.

I decided to speak to them about something we all could identify with: difficult times. I shared my personal struggles of my son passing away and the heartaches that accompanied those trying times. I ended with the power of Jesus to carry us through mountains and valleys.

Afterward, during the greeting period, one elderly man and I talked about several things. He shared the heartache of losing his longtime wife. I could sense his genuine love, not only for Christ, but also for others.

He firmly shook my hand, looked me directly in the eyes, and with a stern face said, "I just want you to know that I love you."

Taken by surprise, I smiled and returned his gesture. "I love you, too."

His face formed an expression of concern. He finally confided, "When I told you I loved you, I wasn't smiling. But when you said you loved me, you were smiling."

"Oh," I responded softly. I repeated my words, but this time with the same sternness he demonstrated.

Weeks later he sent me a card in the mail, offering kind words and best wishes. I replied by sending him a card with best wishes and an ending sure to bring a grin to his face. I ended the card with these words:

"I just want you to know that I love you, and I'm not smiling!"

***

White & Black Challenges

Someone said, "When I look at my family photos, I want to see people all the same color!"

I responded, "Go into your closet and tell me what you see. Different colors, shapes, and sizes. Look at your flower bed, garden, and the interior of your home, what do you see? Go outside and look up at the sky at sunrise or sunset and look at the fields around your home. What do you see?"

Most people are in awe of how different colors, shapes, and sizes blend to form a breathtaking view. But those same people can become bland and homogenous when it comes to the color of humans. God's greatest creation, humans are worth far more than flowers, the sky, and wardrobes."

Sadly, some people have been taught to value and appreciate different colors when it comes to nature but have been consciously and subconsciously taught to devalue and even hate the different colors of human beings.

As humans, we should never try to limit God to one color when it comes to His human creation. That represents ignorance of God's power and lack of appreciation of God's creativity. In other words, it is called racism.

When it comes to racism, there is plenty of room for growth in all races. The following challenges are given to Whites and Blacks because it will take both races working together to finally conquer racism in America.

White Challenge 1:
Acknowledge the Truth about the Confederacy.

After the South surrendered and the North won the Civil War, years of infighting left devastation across the entire country, especially in southern states, cites, and towns. The once vibrant and exuberant economy so many whites enjoyed was wiped out. Four years of savage wartime destroyed the rich infrastructure along with their social elite status of wealth, power, and privilege.

Also, the southern fear of freed blacks became a reality. In a fallen ravaged south, former slave owners came face-to-face with their former slaves who were now, according to federal law, free men and women.

Brutal war and the loss of everything they cherished did not spur a change in heart for some southern whites. They still believed in racial supremacy and sought, in many ways, to exercise power and domination over blacks. They used the local and state political power structure and voter suppression tactics to firmly keep power in the hands of whites.

Southern supremacists needed methods to keep their core belief of racism alive. They needed a justifiable cause for the war, heroes for the south, and a villain. Soon, a convenient storyline was developed called The Lost Cause which painted the south as a mere victim of an aggressive north. It also exaggerated the greatness of the antebellum south and minimized the horrors of slavery.

The storyline denied slavery as the true cause of the war and insisted it was a disagreement over states' rights. It glamorized southern leaders and southern life leading to many confederate statues and confederate names of buildings, schools, and military bases.

Concepts and ideas of The Lost Cause made their way into southern literature and textbooks that were used to educate whites and eventually, blacks about the south and the Civil War. Thus, many whites and blacks received a slanted southern version of history that was not accurate.

Even today, some of our white brothers and sisters still believe confederate statues and the rebel flag are their heritage— symbols of the greatness of the south and historical items to be cherished and revered. They are not aware of the truth about southern lifestyle, the war, and the people they consider heroes.

The facts are that the North and South had a longstanding disagreement about states' rights that involved things such as taxes, slavery, and other issues. But the main concern for southern slave owners was the continuance of slavery because its labor was the cornerstone of the wealth of the south. Without it, they feared the collapse of the southern economy and a loss of their social elite status.

When Southerners lost the balance of power in Congress, there was a steady stream of federal laws passed that were antislavery in nature and meant to limit the influence and spread of slave labor. Some northerners, such as Abolitionists, considered slavery to be immoral, but other northern whites simply feared the competition of cheap slave labor from the south.

As Natives were forced from their land, huge labor opportunities opened. Northern whites found themselves competing with the cheap slave labor from southern slave owners. Thus, slavery was a moral and economic issue for Northerners, and it was the lifeblood of the wealth and social fabric of the South.

When Southern political leaders failed to pass federal laws protecting states' rights to own slaves and advance them into developing territories, they decided to break away from the United States of America and form their own nation—The Confederate States of America.

The South struck first by attacking fort Sumter near Charleston, South Carolina. The federal fort was guarded by Union soldiers. In doing so, the Confederates confiscated the property that officially belonged to the federal government. That was an act of treason by the South and the North responded with a series of counterattacks. After the war, some southern leaders were tried for the crime of treason and served time in prison.

In summary, what the South did was illegal, and the resulting false narrative of The Lost Cause did not paint an accurate picture of the horrors of slaves nor the real reasons for the war.

Now, over 150 years after the war, some southerners need to acknowledge the truth about the antebellum south and the role of slavery in the war.

The antebellum south was not a great period of American history. It was one of the worst times in American history that was filled with sinful and dehumanizing acts toward Blacks and

Natives. African Americans were captured or purchased in Africa and brought to America where they suffered greatly. The Natives were also undergoing attacks from the North and South, and were being killed, sickened by foreign diseases carried by European settlers, and systematically forced from their native lands.

Unfortunately, white supremacy was the core belief of many southerners and the cornerstone of the Confederacy. The rebel flag designers even used the color white to symbolize white supremacy and white purity. Here are portions of a famous speech by Alexander H. Stephens, Vice President of the Confederate States of America.

His speech is called "The Cornerstone Speech" because he painted white supremacy as the cornerstone of their new government, the Confederacy. He used biblical scriptures (Psalms 118:22) and argued that African Americans were morally bound to slavery. He made clear the major reason for the formation of the confederacy, and that reason was white supremacy and slavery.

> *"Our new government is founded upon exactly the opposite ideas; its foundations are laid, its cornerstone rests, upon the great truth that the negro is not equal to the white man; that slavery, subordination to the superior race, is his natural and normal condition. This, our new government, is the first, in the history of the world, based upon this great physical, philosophical, and moral truth. This truth has been slow in the process of its development, like all other truths in the various departments of science."*
>
> *(https://en.wikipedia.org/wiki/Cornerstone_Speech)*

His fiery speech was given just weeks before the Civil War on March 21, 1861 at the Athenaeum in Savannah, Georgia. After the war ended, he attempted to retract his statements made in the speech by denying slavery was the cause for the Confederacy's formation and secession from the Union.

But given his words, can there be any doubt about the foundational beliefs of the Confederate States of America? The formation of the Confederate States of America had two major driving factors: its belief in white supremacy and its insistence on states' rights to own black slaves.

The challenge to my white brothers and sisters is to acknowledge the truth about the past of the confederacy. Only the truth can bring healing in America.

Heritage vs. History

There are many white decedents of confederate soldiers or southern slave owners who feel the need to honor and carry on the memories of their confederate ancestors. While that is understandable, remembering ancestors should be done in a way that acknowledges their existence without glorifying and perpetuating their wrong beliefs and actions.

Some consider the confederacy as their heritage and that removing statues and the confederate flags are attempts to destroy their past and rewrite history.

History is a set of facts that occurred in the past. But confederate history was not told the way it happened. That leads to perverted stories such as The Lost Cause which, in effect, causes people in the present to live by lies of the past.

In this case, the story needs to be rewritten and the true version of history should be heard and disseminated to all future generations so they can know the truth.

Yes, telling the truth about the confederacy is rewriting history. The false narrative of the glorious and patriotic south that was only defending itself from an aggressive north should be retold.

There are also some white brothers and sisters who feel their heritage is under attack. Heritage is something passed on to the present generation by ancestors. The present generation has the choice to accept what is passed on or reject it. Supremacy and racism passed on by the ancestors of the south, don't have to be part of the present generation unless it is believed, embraced, and practiced.

If you are a white confederate descendent, do you believe, embrace, and practice the confederate mindset of racial supremacy? If you do, then those ignorant, bigoted, and sinful beliefs are your heritage because you accepted them. Is that the heritage you are proud of and are anxious to pass to your children?

My father, grandfather, and many other family members were part of a certain secret organization. Access to this group was passed down from generation to generation. After researching the organization, I did not believe some of its practices were consistent with Christian teachings. When I was in my twenties, I was invited by my older sibling to speak at the organization. After my speech, leaders asked me to become a member.

I kindly rejected their offer because I did not want to accept its practices as part of my heritage. The challenge for some southern white brothers and sisters is to reject the white supremacy beliefs of their ancestors and the glorification of symbols of racism and discrimination.

Yes, they were your ancestors, but their wrong beliefs and practices do not have to become your inheritance—unless that is what you want. And if it is what you want, why do you embrace something you know in your heart is wrong?

Parents should be the gatekeepers for the family. Gatekeepers should only allow integrity and truth to enter the family and become part of its heritage. The challenge is not to allow the lie of white supremacy to become ingrained in your family's beliefs. If you do, you will leave it for your children or grandchildren to fight.

You can and should be the agent of change needed to halt the effects of generations of false beliefs. The challenge is to stand up and be the good gatekeeper. I believe you can and will.

White Challenge 2:
Become Involved in Social Justice.

During the civil rights movement in America, Dr. Martin Luther King, Jr. once said, "In the end, we will remember not the words of our enemies, but the silence of our friends."

At that time, there were many good white people who disagreed with supremacy, racism, and discrimination, but who, for various reasons, chose to remain silent. They refused to speak up on the behalf of the many blacks who were mistreated. They failed to oppose their white family and friends who held racists beliefs and committed discriminatory practices.

They did not march, protest, or otherwise bring any atten-tion to the injustice that occurred around them. For many, they did not want to rock-the-boat or create conflict even if that con-flict was for a righteous cause. Perhaps comfort and privilege were more important that justice and equality. Perhaps they suf-fered from overwhelming fear and lacked the courage to confront evil. Whatever the issue may have been, they failed the civil rights movement and in turn indirectly aided the spread and dominance of racial supremacy.

People below the age of fifty, more than likely, were not involved in the height of the civil rights movement in America that occurred in the 1960s. For those people, now is the time to become involved in the modern struggle for justice and equal-ity. Speak up. Speak out. Join some social justice group and raise your voice for positive change.

Learn more about the history of African Americans, Na-tives, and other minorities. Seek understanding and become informed about the injustices of yesterday and compare them to the injustices of today. Become a part of the solution to rac-ism and not merely a silent bystander unwilling to make sacrifices or give up the conveniences of white privilege. Learn the lessons of history.

For those who were around during the decade of the 1960s and did not join the struggle, now is your time for redemption. You can correct the inaction of your past by becoming active in the present. You can join the movement by participating in peaceful marches and protests. You can give to social justice causes and groups. You can speak up and speak out. And you can be the gatekeeper of your home by correcting the inaccurate version of history spread by The Lost Cause.

The challenge is to do something positive and right. Help your brothers and sisters in your home country and around the world, usher in an era of justice and equality. Leave a heritage of a righteous legacy for your descendants.

White Challenge 3:
Practice ALL the Gospel

History suggests the teachings of Christianity came to England by way of France around the fourth century. That means the English descendants who fled England and landed in America around 1620 had the gospel in their possession for over thirteen centuries or 1,300 years.

Despite having the infallible Word of God and the powerful teachings of Jesus Christ, some of those same people and their descendants committed or allowed the enslavement of Africans. They did not follow Christianity in its fullness. Instead, some of them perverted and used the Word of God to justify their horrific treatment of other humans created in the image of God.

If some of the pilgrims and their descendants had lived out the full gospel, the indigenous Natives of America would not have been systematically killed and driven from their homelands. If most of them had truly known and feared the God of the Bible, the horrendous slave trade would not have taken place.

If most of their descendants truly believed in the righteousness of God, they would have helped the former black slaves build their lives after the Civil War. Instead, many placed stumbling blocks in the path of blacks on every turn. That was not the full gospel.

Now, in 2020, the Word of God has been in the hands of European English descendants for over 1,700 years. And still, white supremacy and racism continue to be major issues among the community of our white brothers and sisters and of other races. How long does it take to practice something before finally mastering it?

How long does it take to perfect loving your neighbor as yourself? How long does it take to learn to do unto others as you would have them do unto you?

That was a lesson many white brothers and sisters did not learn and did not practice as proven by their mistreatment of natives and blacks. And sadly, even today, there seems to be a disconnect that some whites and blacks have when it comes to practicing the love one another scriptures of the Bible. This has allowed supremacy and racism to replicate throughout the centuries.

Therefore, the white challenge in this area is to be true to the faith. Live out the fullness of the gospel of Jesus Christ and perfect the love of others as the Word of God instructs.

When we all live out the fullness of the gospel, supremacy and racism will die because it does not have any fear and hatred to feed on. When a person is true to the entire Word of God, his or her light of righteousness will shine forth as the Sun in its strength. And all of God's people will live together in peace and harmony.

Black Challenge 1:
Create a Safe Place for Racial Conversations.

I am fully convinced blacks and other minorities cannot solve the issues of racism alone. It will take agreement and cooperation from all races.

Since the George Floyd killing, many whites have joined the cause for racial justice and equality in record numbers. So have Hispanics, Asians, Natives, and others. The multicolored rainbows of individuals who were present at marches and protests around the world was a welcomed sight for the movement. It demonstrated the expansive awareness of injustice in America by those on several continents.

Despite this, blacks must continue to make concerted efforts to cross over the racial wall and appeal to their white counterparts and others about racial injustice and equality. But the challenge is not only to reach out but to do so in the most constructive manner.

That means, as blacks, we should continue to talk about and challenge others on the issues of racism by creating a safe place for tough conversations. That includes believing others can add value to the hard issue of racism and could have similar experiences and struggles.

There are some white people who have experienced discriminatory acts although it may not have been a lifetime of occurrences as is typical with most blacks. But that person's experience should count for something.

The challenge for blacks in this area is to reach out beyond the racial wall and make others feel like participators in the conversation.

There needs to be a safe place created for all races to share their true experiences, thoughts, and opinions without the fear of being dismissed or discounted.

It is up to us as blacks to create that safe space for difficult conversations and to invite others to participate. Then we can speed up the arrival of true healing among the races.

Black Challenge 2:
See Whites as Individuals

Sometimes it is easy to assume all white people are descendants of former slave owners. Some conversations can be fashioned in a way that makes that assumption. I recently read an online posting from a minority who laid out everything white people needed to do to correct racism. It was pointed, harsh, and highly accusatory. It hurt me to read it, so I could imagine the hurt and pain it may have caused a white reader.

I believe most African Americans know that all whites are not racists. But there are times when their choice of words may not reflect that fact. As a race, we are passionate, and perhaps that explains some situations where opinions are expressed with vitriol. But we should be careful of using broad paint brushes to paint everyone a certain way.

For example, everyone who fought for the Confederacy were not racists. The suggestion that they were is an example of paint-brushing. Many southerners did fight to keep slaves, but there were some who joined for other reasons.

Historical accounts of diaries and journals of some who fought for the Confederacy reveal some of the reasons they joined. One reason was the fear of losing their home, land, and other valuables. There were some Southerners who did not own slaves nor wished to own slaves. But they did love their lifestyle and feared it would be taken if the South lost the war.

It would be worthwhile to read about Confederate soldier John S Mosby who fought for the South but disagreed with slavery. His justification was:

> *"I am not ashamed of having fought on the side of slavery – a soldier fights for his country – right or wrong – he is not responsible for the political merits of the cause he fights in. The South was my country."*
>
> *https://www.gilderlehrman.org/history-resources/spotlight-primary-source/former-confederate-officer-slavery-and-civil-war-1907?gclid=Cj0KCQjwtMCKBhDAARIsAG-2Eu9HlOxp687pkOw09vcOj6AACnAXZNNo9Zuo-yJAGv5x11Qc5lQgo34oaAnr9EALw_wcB*

In an earlier chapter, I discussed the meaning of supremacy (belief that one's race is superior), racism (belief that one's race should be separated), and unconscious bias (learned untruths about race).

A person who simply has an unconscious bias is not a racist. All people have unconscious bias. Therefore, we should be cautious when labeling a person as a racist.

As mentioned previously, most people who only have an unconscious bias will eventually accept the truth while it is usually more difficult to convince a supremacist or racist.

In this world where social media takes information around the globe in a matter of seconds, someone's life can be ruined by an online accusation or video clip gone viral.

Black Challenge 3:
Open the Umbrella of Justice

In 2020, the fight for racial justice and equality caught fire. Suddenly, people, groups, and companies in America and around the world appear to have experienced a social justice awakening. Stars are reaching out to blacks in multiple ways— offering a helping hand to assist in boosting notoriety for black causes.

Companies are enacting racially sensitive changes and investing in social justice organizations. Even policies and laws are being put in place as chants of "No Justice, No Peace" continue to ring out.

That is great for the movement. But during all the excitement about the awakening, let us not forget those other races who have suffered for long periods with the beasts of racism and inequality.

Let us not forget our Native brothers and sisters, our Jewish and Muslim communities, our Hispanic and Asian members, and others. Let us extend a helping hand to them as we continue to fight the good fight of faith. Let us march with them when they protest. Let us mourn with them when they are attacked. Let us use some of our newfound notoriety and influence to make their struggles known. Let us use some of our resources to aid them in a time of need.

I am convinced that as blacks who have greatly suffered for over 400 years, we will not leave those behind who are experiencing the same injustice.

Black Challenge 4:
Acknowledge Black Racism

Blacks can be and sometimes are, racist. I realize that is a loaded statement that will bring much backlash from many in the black community. But I am the seventeenth son of poor farmers and have hundreds of relatives—a few of which are racists. They are separation racist in the sense that they do not believe in interracial dating or marriage.

As a minister who has conducted private biblical counseling sessions for years, I can certainly say I have counseled black people with racist mindsets.

One famous black author wrote that black people cannot be racist because they do not possess the power needed to control vital institutions of society. But I believe being a racist has nothing to do with the power one does or does not possess. I believe it is a state of mind that anyone can have and thus is independent of what position or power a person holds.

Here are a few personal examples of black racism that I have either experienced, heard about, or read about.

Black against White Racism

I will change his name to William. He was a white coworker with whom I had the pleasure of working with for nearly twenty years.

He was a pure country boy born and raised on a farm in South Alabama. He was an older white man who loved square-dancing, horses, and his family. Over the years we became very close. There were times when he confided some deep personal situations to me and even asked me to pray for him.

His language was pure southern-boy-country. He used the word "boy" when talking to everyone, including blacks and whites. He had a style of communication that at times, could be taken out of context and viewed as racist. But everyone knew him too well to think he was racist. That is, until a new black coworker joined the company.

I was familiar with the new hire and knew he had a problem with white people. William was a team leader and the new hire was placed under him. A few months later, things began to get bad between them. The new hire accused William of being a racist and deliberately giving him a bad work review.

He filed several complaints to Human Resources about William over the course of a few months. But the final breaking point was when William, using his usual speaking style, used the word "boy" when talking to the new hire. Not like, "Hey you boy." More like, "Boy, what you think about that?"

The new hire went to Human Resources and filed a complaint stating that William called him a boy and that was offensive language to him. Human Resources called William into the office to hear his side of the story.

Days after his office visit, William came to me. I heard what happened and tried to encourage him to hang in there. "Charlie, if they call you in, will you vouch for me?" William asked.

"Sure, I will William." I said. "You are a lot of things, but racist is not one of them."

We laughed.

About one week later he shared the bad news with me. The company had decided his fate. They gave him a choice to retire early or be terminated. He was devastated and I felt awful for him.

"Maybe I can talk to them." I suggested.

"No Charlie." He replied. "It is too late. I already told them I would retire. He shared his deep disappointment that a person could work for a company for over twenty years with a clean record. Yet, when one person complains about racism, the company can overreact and throw a person to the wolves.

I was very hurt and distraught about how things played out with William. On his last day we all said our goodbyes and when he and I embraced, I could see tears welling up in his eyes. For a moment, I too felt the hurt and pain caused by labeling an innocent person a racist. This time, it was caused by someone in my own race. I wanted to apologize to him for what someone in my race had done to unjustly end his career. But I know William would have said, "Don't apologize. You didn't do anything."

But in a way, I felt I had done something horrible and unjust. It is somewhat like watching your sibling do something wrong to another person. You know it wasn't you, but some guilt may surface because it was your sibling who did it.

For the first time, I somewhat understood how some white people may feel when they are accused of being a racist purely based on their skin color. It was not a good feeling.

What helped me finally let it go was seeing William a few years later at a retirement party for another coworker. We embraced and talked for a long time. He seemed very happy and content. He even said that hurtful situation worked out for his good.

I breathed a sigh of relief and finally shook that sickening feeling of being dirty. But that incident brought something ugly about my race to the forefront of my mind. It had been something I didn't want to think about or admit—that some black people are racist too. And their racist acts can also ruin lives and cause great harm.

Thankfully, that time, all turned out okay. But what about the countless experiences some whites have that do not turn out well?

Black against Black Racism

Years ago, a black friend started a cleaning company and worked hard over the years to build it into a successful competing business. He eventually sold his business to a larger competitor and moved his small black cleaning crew under the mostly white workforce of the larger company. He was now doing business as that larger organization.

The organization assigned his cleaning team to work at a certain facility where the larger company had previously negotiated the contract. After several cleanings, he heard that one of the high-level facility managers, a black person, was unhappy with his cleaning team.

He did not understand why. The team had done a great job and had not received any work-related complaints from anyone else. Curious, he spoke with the manager to determine the issue. After the black manager refused to name any specific cleaning problem, the manager dropped this bombshell of a statement.

"I thought your company was white."

Completely shocked, my friend managed to pull himself together and explain how his cleaning team came under the umbrella of the larger organization. A short time later, his cleaning team was taken off the assignments for that facility. No reasonable explanation given.

He surmised it was a racial issue based on the black manager's statement and no accusation of performance problems.

That was not the first racist incident my friend encountered in his line of business. But that was the first incident where a black person had committed the racist offense. That shocked him the most.

Truthfully, there are many black against black racist acts that occur in other ways. But this fact is something most people in the black community do not willingly admit or openly discuss. Here are some of the ways blacks have contributed to slavery and racism in the past.

As Slave Sellers:

African kings, chiefs, and leaders sold other blacks to slave buyers during the Trans-Atlantic slave trade. The exact number of slaves provided by blacks is unknown, but slave traders could not have been as successful without the assistance of African slave sellers.

As Slave Owners:

Some blacks also owned black slaves in the American south during the Antebellum period prior to the Civil War. They were few and most accounts of black slave owners were linked to what I call "mercy" ownership. Meaning free blacks were attempting to secure freedom of family members and others by temporarily owning them. It was an attempt to protect them from the horrors of some white slave owners.

But there are some accounts of black slave owners being as ruthless and harsh on black slaves as some of the worst white slave owners.

As Slave Trackers:

Imagine being a slave and you risk everything, including your very life, to run away. Days later you are tracked down and dragged back to the plantation to face a painful punishment or even death. To make things worse, one of the people who tracked you down and forcefully brought you back was black!

Black slave trackers were few, but they did exist. They assisted white trackers in hunting down escaped slaves. The reason was age-old: Money. In those days the capture of a few black slaves could bring enough money for a free black person to buy a house, land, or start a business. It was unconscionable, but none-the-less true.

As Confederate Soldiers or Supporters:

It may be hard to believe why some blacks fought for and supported the Southern Confederate cause, but the reasons are simple. Some blacks were taken into the confederate military by their masters where they served in various capacities such as cook, labor, or bodyguard.

Some free blacks who had good and decent livelihoods, feared whatever they owned would be taken by those in the North. They assisted the South during the war in various ways including monetarily.

Also, some black slaves had good relationships with their masters and the family and were willing to help the Southern confederate cause. Perhaps they thought life outside of what they already had would be worse if the South lost the war.

How do we deal with these unpleasant truths as black people? Do we shy away from them? Explain them away or refuse to acknowledge their existence?

We must confront them head-on because we cannot conquer what we refuse to confront.

As black people we must also rid ourselves of the racist language and epitaphs we use against each other. Labels and words such as:

Uncle Tom: (Mostly used pre-1970s)

A racist term meaning a black person with a slave mentality. One who is afraid of whites and caters to their every need.

House Ni**er: (Mostly used pre-1970s)

A derogatory term that means a black person who has it good by sucking up to white people.

Ni**er:

A demeaning term that was once listed in the dictionary to mean worthless, no-good, lazy, and black among other definitions. Even today, some blacks continue to use the word as a term of endearment toward other blacks in their music, poetry, and communication.

I am a firm believer that no matter how some blacks use that word to supposedly mean good, their use of it will never overshadow the truth of why it was created: to demean and humiliate black people.

High-Yellow: (Mostly used pre-1970s)

A black racial slur used by some blacks to indicate not black enough or not pure black based on a person's skin tone.

In an episode of the comedy Sanford and Son, Fred plays the role of a racist black man who opposed the dating of his son and a Mexican girl. Fred tells the girl's mother, "If she (your daughter) likes our people (black people), let her start at the bottom. Let her start with a high-yellow and work up!"

Skin-but-not-Kin:

A derogatory phrase that means a black person who does not have the commonly accepted political or social mindset of most blacks. This term is often used in the political arena to indicate a black person who does not support traditionally black agendas such as civil rights, racial equality, and equal justice.

How can we, as blacks, continually say to others, "Stop judging me by my skin tone," if we do the same to ourselves?

It can be hard to accept the truth about black involvement in slavery and racism. But we should ponder these facts in our hearts and finally arrive at a bitter-sweet conclusion.

As blacks, we have been both providers and recipients of misery. Slave owners and slaves. Oppressors and the oppressed. These facts are very complicated.

However, we must, as a race of black people, call out the racist acts in our own community along with the racist acts of others.

White & Black Challenge 1:

Forgive From the Heart

In a previous chapter, I talked about true forgiveness. This goes for both whites and blacks. Whites need to forgive those blacks who have hurt them by mistakenly calling them racists. That can be extremely hurtful and can result in bitterness and distrust of African Americans. It can also cause some whites to shut down when it comes to discussing racial issues.

From the heart means, I will not hold your mistake against you. As much as you can, chalk that person's bad decision up to their lack of knowing you. Give that person the opportunity to change his or her mind as they become more familiar with your experiences and opinions.

Blacks should forgive the past actions of slave owners and their current descendants—even if the current descendants still believe in white supremacy and racism. Forgiveness should cover the past and the present.

Blacks should also forgive their African ancestors for the role they played in the slave trade. The transport of millions of slaves from Africa to America could not have happened in such large numbers without the participation of African leaders.

When whites and blacks practice true forgiveness, they can participate in tough racial conversations in a respectful manner—free of anger and hostility. There cannot be true healing of the races without true forgiveness on both sides.

White & Black Challenge 2:
Rock the Church Boat!

He was the second-generation Alabama Pastor of a white congregation. His father, during the height of the civil rights movement, preached racial supremacy and separation as the will of God. He did not believe in white supremacy or racism, but he saw no advantage in preaching or teaching on racism in the white congregation he pastored because he feared upsetting the people.

In his famous letter from the Birmingham jail, Martin Luther King, Jr. argued that church leaders needed to take their mission of preaching about social justice seriously and he referenced the failure of "white churchmen" to stand up for racial justice. He wrote:

> *So often the contemporary church is a weak, ineffectual voice with an uncertain sound, so often it is an arch-defender of the status quo. Far from being disturbed by the presence of the church, the power structure of the average community is consoled by the church's silent — and often even vocal — sanction of things as they are.*

Martin said something that needs to be reiterated today — that too many white church leaders are comfortable with the status quo of racism among their own congregations and are often too afraid to challenge their parishioners' beliefs on supremacy and racism.

They are fearful of rocking the church boat and cower at the prospect of upsetting the political power players who serve in leadership and financially support the ministry.

But honestly, black church leaders could stand some improvement in this area as well. As a black congregant, I realize black leaders often preach and teach on racial injustice. But I believe we should teach it from a racial reconciliation aspect as well as a social injustice aspect.

We should preach and teach on forgiving those who enslaved our forefathers and on how to heal the races. Saying injustice is wrong is the correct message. But it is also necessary to promote healing and unity through forgiveness. The body of Christ needs leaders who are not afraid to rock the church boat.

Churches tend to operate within a cultural context, but leaders still need to challenge those cultures and compare them to the Word of God. Only then can the church overcome supremacy and racism and grow into the mature body that Christ is looking for upon His return.

White & Black Challenge 3:
Acknowledge Race Cards

It was my first real job as an assembly line auditor in the early 1980s. One of my coworkers was an older black man who had lived through the turbulent times of the 1960s civil rights movement. On several occasions he indicated his distrust for whites.

Our manager was an older white man born and raised in a rural area of Alabama that was known for its racist reputation. Despite that fact, the manager's actions and words always seemed straight-forward and fair, at least to me. But to my coworker, our manager always seemed to say or suggest something racist even when it came to asking simple questions.

"He got no right approaching me like that!" My coworker often said. Somewhere in his complaints and accusations, the words "he's a racist" often fell from his lips. But complaining was just part of my coworker's actions. He also went to upper management and all the way to the Vice President of operations with his claims of racism and injustice.

One day I was working on my line when another manager came to my area. "Charlie, the Big Cheese wants to see you in his office. The Vice President sent me to get you. What did you do?"

I swallowed. "I don't know. But I guess I'll find out."

I walked the five-minute journey that seemed like an hour and finally stepped inside the Vice President's office. The secretary greeted me. "Go right in Charlie. He's expecting you."

I opened the door and saw three people sitting around a conference table. All of them were senior executives—two white men and one black man.

"What the hell is this all about?" I pondered.

"Charlie," the Vice President said as he extended his hand in my direction, "come on around and have a seat."

I walked nervously to the table and gingerly sat beside him. "I know you are wondering what this is about." He said as the other executives peered at me.

"Yes," I responded, "that crossed my mind."

"Don't worry," he said, "there is nothing wrong. We just need to ask you a few questions about your manager."

A frown appeared on my face.

"We have been told that your manager has said some things and acted in some ways that are racist toward black people," he continued, "and we wanted to ask you if you have experienced or heard anything from him that you consider to be racist."

I sat back in the seat and took a few seconds to collect my thoughts.

"No. I can't say he has said or done anything to me that I would consider racist. I mean, he is an older guy from a very guarded town and sometimes he can be a little blunt and border on insensitive, but nothing racist from my point of view."

We all continued to chat for about ten minutes and afterwards I made my way back to my floor position.

A few days later my black coworker approached me. "Man," he said with a huge hint of disappointment in his voice, "they not going to do anything about our manager. They said you didn't have any issues with him and did not think he was racist."

I nodded my head in agreement to his summation and continued to do my work.

"Why didn't you back me up?" He asked. "Why didn't you say he was racist?"

I stopped my work and turned to look at him. "Because I don't think he is a racist. He has not done anything to me."

Unhappy with my response, my coworker walked away in disgust. We managed to stay on talking terms, but I could sense there was always something standing between us.

About ten years later, as I worked for another company, a similar situation happened. A black coworker accused our manager, a white female, of being a racist. He bitterly complained to Human Resources and there I was again, sitting in the hot seat, and talking to the Human Resource Director.

Again, I explained that I did not have an issue with our manager and did not think she was a racist. In fact, I told my black coworker that when our manager discovered he did not have the training or knowledge to perform certain assignments, she did not fire him. Instead, she sent him to be trained—free of charge. Racists don't do that.

But he still insisted and even accused other white leaders of the same. He eventually left the company—parting on very bitter terms.

I have heard some white brothers and sisters use the phrase, "playing the race card." When I first heard it years before these two incidents, I cringed at the sound of those words and even became defensive toward white people who uttered them. But sadly, I must admit, that some black people do play the race card to either get what they want or to gain some advantage.

However, that does not dismiss the many legitimate complaints, experiences, and observations of racism that many blacks encounter daily. And blacks are not the only race with "race cards" to play. Some of my white brothers and sisters do the same. Here is a personal story about the "white privilege" race card.

I will change my black friend's name to Javon. Years ago, he ran for public office. He was a republican and had supported many republicans for years through donations and volunteering for various campaigns. He confessed to me that he thought republicans had accepted him and that his race meant nothing negative. But when he ran for office against a white republican, he discovered how sinister some white people could become.

Weeks before Election Day, some polls showed Javon leading his white republican counterpart. That's when it all started—the "white privilege" race card came out.

Some white republicans wanted his counterpart to win and made phone calls to white voters to sway their vote. That alone is not racist. But it was what some of them said that invoked the white privilege race card.

"Javon reminds me of Obama...smart and articulate."

They said other racial statements that I will omit. But I want you to understand how comparing a candidate to then President Barack Obama, in the south, was a racist game plan. It is called southern strategy and the goal is to use racial undertones in a negative way to gain advantage in a race.

For many southern whites, former President Barack Obama represented the very thing many of them feared for centuries— race mixing. Mr. Obama's African-English-Iris heritage, along with his liberal beliefs, made him extremely unpopular in most Southern states. Javon was black so it was easy to establish a mental connection between him and Obama.

At the height of the chatter, Javon called upon a few republicans who were not involved. One republican official called people who were discrediting Javon--telling them to knock it off. But it was too little too late. Javon lost the election. Some white people assisting Javon's campaign were even threatened during the height of the chatter. One white woman helping Javon was so frightened that she moved her family to another state.

As he relayed his experience to me, I could see the surprise and disbelief stamped across his face. "How could they do this to me after all the support I gave them?" He asked.

I listened and tried to encourage him to run again in the future. I didn't say this to him, but I concluded that not only do some blacks play the race card, but some whites do also. Both can use their race to obtain some advantage or to get what they want.

Therefore, I say this to both my black and white brothers and sisters. Please put away the race cards that are so easily accessible. The victim race card. The privilege race card. And any others that may be floating around. And let us determine not to seek or gain unfair advantage over anyone because of the color of our skin.

All Races Challenge:
Stand Up to Racism

She was a sweetheart of a neighbor. A charming older white woman who lived close to our home many years ago. She and her husband were very helpful to anyone who needed assistance. That is why I couldn't believe what she said about Mexicans.

One day three of us neighbors were leaning against the fence in our backyard, talking about various things in the neighborhood. One small house next to my older neighbor had been vacated and she happened to see a group of people come to check out the house.

The people were Mexican. "You know," she said in the midst of a string of other statements, "looks like some Mexican's came to look at the house next to us."

My other neighbor and I said nothing. We both nodded our heads to her news.

"You know they sleep on top of each other..."

My face dropped and as I glanced at my other neighbor who was a middle-age white female, her face reflected the shock I was experiencing. Neither of us said anything to our older neighbor. We merely cut the conversation short and walked back to our home.

Afterwards, I felt guilty for not saying anything to show disapproval of her statement. After all, I saw her as my own mother and concluded it was best to just let it go. I figured nothing I said would have made a difference.

Maybe that is the point. Sometimes we ponder speaking up because we think it will not change the person. But maybe we should speak up to simply show our disapproval and make people uncomfortable showing their racism in our presence.

As I write and update this book, our Asian brothers and sisters are undergoing tremendous attacks from people of many races, including blacks. The Covid-19 pandemic false rumors and statements aimed at blaming Asians for the virus have led to fierce verbal and physical attacks. Some are happening in broad daylight and captured on camera for all the world to witness.

What should be our response? Speak up for our Asian brothers and sisters. Protect them, defend them, and love them.

Speaking up does not mean being confrontational. It simply means we should let people know we do not agree with their racist words or acts. Weather the racist acts are:

Bananas thrown on a soccer field

Monkey chants from sports fans

Racist slurs and gestures from fans and players

A hangman's noose on campus, arenas, or the workplace

Racist jokes, comments, or statements

Racist attacks and suggestions in papers, on TV, or online

We all should take a stand and show our disapproval in non-confrontational ways. We can give that person a look of disappointment. We can voice our opinion verbally or in written format. We can share our positive experiences with other races.

Whatever the method, we should do something. If we don't, racists will continue to feel comfortable saying and doing racist things when they should become uncomfortable because they know there is opposition.

That may not change them, but at least they will be put on notice.

Why Blacks Should Celebrate Independence Day

According to ancestry records, my great-great grandfather was born in Virginia and my great grandfather was born in Alabama. Both my parent's ancestors were slaves on the Mooresville Plantation in North Alabama prior to the outbreak of the Civil War. After the war, many in my family decided to stay in North Alabama. Most, like my grandfather and father, worked as sharecroppers for white landowners. My grandfather even served in World War II.

As a descendent of slaves, I often hear the opinion that blacks should not celebrate Independence Day because July 4th did not give slaves their freedom. While that statement is true, I believe there is something else blacks should consider about Independence Day.

There are two types of freedom we enjoy in America. The first type is National Freedom where our nation is not beholden to any other nation. The second type is Personal Freedom where each person or group of people enjoy full citizenship with all rights thereof. It took America two phases to gain both types of freedom. Phase I of National Freedom was declared on July 4th, 1776. Phase II of personal freedom came about after the Emancipation Proclamation and culminated at the end of the Civil War in 1865. On June 19th of 1865, news of slave freedom was delivered to blacks in Texas—better known as Juneteenth.

In freedom Phase I, America won its National Freedom to form its own government, laws, and select its own representatives. With victory, no other Country or nation could place obligations upon America as did England in the 1700's. The outcome of that war determined if America would have a King or a President, national freedom, or national subjugation to England. It was a very important victory for the Colonies as they cast the perfect vision of equality with these words in the Declaration of Independence,

"We hold these truths to be self-evident, that all men are created equal.."

Although it would take seven more years of war to finally gain national independence from England, the perfect vision of *all men are created equal* was not realized in practice. Some sixty-seven thousand slaves were still in bondage in America at that time. In Phase I, National Freedom had been achieved, but there needed to be a Phase II of Personal freedom for slaves to be recognized as American citizens. This discrepancy between perfect vision and imperfect execution was a huge factor that led to the Civil War.

During the war, in 1862, President Abraham Lincoln, as Commander in Chief of the military, drafted the Emancipation

Proclamation, a military order declaring all slaves in Confederate States would be free on January 1st, 1863. An estimated four-million slaves were in bondage at that time and the arrival of January 1st, 1863, brought very little wide-spread personal freedom for slaves. The nation was at war and the confederate states did not recognize Lincoln's authority for such an order.

However, pockets of slaves did manage to escape to nearby Union camps where they found personal freedom and joined the Union Army. The Union army was also able to set slaves free as they captured Confederate towns and cities. Finally, at the end of the war in April 1865, Confederate states were forced to recognize Lincoln's Emancipation Proclamation and millions of slaves suddenly received their Personal Freedom. In Phase II of Personal Freedom, former slaves became citizens in a nation that had previously declared its National Freedom in 1776.

Phase I of National Freedom was not complete without Phase II of Personal Freedom. And Phase II of Personal Freedom would have been incomplete without Phase I of National Freedom. I believe we should celebrate them both because each phase was a step toward the perfect vision that:

"All men (people) are created equal."

Some African Americans may retort, "England offered blacks freedom if they fought for them during the Revolutionary War."

That is true. However, at that time, blacks would have only gained personal freedom in a nation that answered to a King and Queen. In the English government at that time, blacks would not have had significant input, participation, or representation in governmental affairs.

Yes, it took many years in America to gain political participation and representation, but I believe the American system of governance is the best on the face of the earth.

Therefore, as a slave descendant, I celebrate July 4th as National Independence Day. With it, my ancestors and I received a free nation that decides its own fate. And I also celebrate June 19th, Juneteenth, as Phase II of my ancestors Personal Freedom to become citizens with rights thereof, in what I consider to be the greatest Nation on Earth.

To me, celebrating one without the other is not an option. I must celebrate both because total freedom can only be found in a nation with National freedom among a people who have Personal Freedom. On July 4th, I will sing, dance, and celebrate along with all others who recognize and appreciate the tremendous sacrifice of the founders of this great nation called America.

Therefore, on June 19th, let us all celebrate Juneteenth, Phase II of Personal Freedom delivered by the Emancipation Proclamation. And on July 4th, let us all celebrate Independence Day, Phase I of National Freedom. In fact, let us celebrate them both.

Happy Juneteenth and Happy Independence Day from a slave descendent.

Four: Self-Evaluation & Discussion

Think about YOUR race or race mixture only. Which challenges have you witnessed with your race?

Which challenges do you agree with? Which do you disagree with?

What race cards have you seen played by either blacks or whites?

What other points would you want to group-discuss in this chapter?

CHAPTER FIVE

The Assimilation Mindset

he historic town of Mooresville, AL., is home to a tiny
two-room dilapidated shack that still stands, but slumps
near a weathered fence. That two-room tiny wonder
served as the dwelling place in the 1940s for my mother and
her first four children.

I was not supposed to be born, at least according to my
momma's account of my arrival into the world. In 1963, a year
prior to my birth, my father already had a total of sixteen children—seven from a previous marriage, and nine from the union
with my mother.

But for some strange reason, he had an insatiable appetite
for one more child. But momma, close to forty years old and
having suffered nine grueling at-home deliveries, firmly decided to go into childbearing retirement and collect her
"company pension."

That set the stage for numerous verbal confrontations.
Momma was about half the size of my father. She stood a mea-
sly 5 feet 4 inches and barely tipped the scales at 100 pounds
soaking wet holding two bricks. But on this issue, she stood her
verbal ground and refused to be intimidated.

During heated arguments, she marched up to my father, spread her tiny legs for leverage, threw her head back, and delivered the breaking news, "The next baby born in this house gon come from your belly!"

(Go women!)

My father, after several unsuccessful attempts to persuade her, resorted to plan B of pathetic, manly begging. Weeks later, she miraculously conceded and nine months later, I came into the world kicking and screaming—the seventeenth child of my father and tenth child of my mother.

A few years after my birth in the 1960s, my grandfather came to live with us after the death of my grandmother. We were already cramped as we packed eleven people into a small, five-room blockhouse. My father moved us around and managed to give my grandfather his own room. My grandfather was a WWI vet who talked to a German helmet he kept in his room as he recanted wartime incidents to himself.

He was known as a stingy man. My mother often retold a story about him eating moldy bread because he simply refused to spend money on fresh bread. His words, made famous by my mother, were, "Mold or no mold, I'm gon' eat this bread."

He collected social security checks but failed to cash many of them—rendering them of no value due to their expiration dates. Many times, he could have helped our family buy the essentials of food and clothing, but he simply refused. This was also the case concerning any family member's emergency health care needs—including the needs of his own son who took him in and cared for him.

For years my father suffered from something my mother called spells. Later in life, I realized they were really seizures. He violently trembled and shook during those incidents and even injured himself at times. Those horrible episodes usually lasted only a few minutes, but his final seizure lasted much longer.

I was only five years old, and I could hear my father's torturous screams of pain. I tried to shield myself from his agonizing cries by covering my ears with my hands and pressing down with all my might. My mother's tear-soaked face revealed the deep helplessness and despair she must have felt as she held him tightly, trying to ease his pain by holding a cold wet cloth on his forehead.

My older siblings tried for hours to convince my grandfather to give them money to take my father to the emergency room, but he sternly and coldly refused. Finally, my siblings decided to take desperate action.

They forced their way into my grandfather's room and began to search the place—despite his protests—looking for his stash of money. They found his money, took a portion of it, and rushed my father to the hospital.

A short time afterward a family member brought us the news about my father's condition—telling us, "Your father is dead."

My grandfather cried like a baby. I thought his tears were for the death of his son until these mumbling words fell from his lips: "My money. My money."

After my father's death, my mother moved the family into a small, dilapidated house owned by a black family. She did not want to continue to live in the white landlord's house. The loss of my father's income meant everyone in the family had to make money and chip in. Momma could not afford to be a stay-at-home mom and did whatever was necessary to help feed and clothe her family.

During strawberry season, she picked for hours on bended knees and pushed and pulled heavy trays from end to end of the field. At the end of many exhausting days, she rubbed her legs and arms down with alcohol to relieve the aches.

Through it all, she complained very little about the difficult work, the horrific conditions, or the meager pay. Instead, she sang and hummed her way through those strenuous times.

She loved to sing and was a member of the church choir. She often bellowed out songs as she worked in the fields, cleaned in the house, or cultivated in the garden. She used songs as a way of expressing her hurt and happiness.

As I played one day, I saw her in the kitchen humming and making cornbread. I saw tears rolling down her face as she whipped the batter. She hummed the tunes of sad songs. I gazed upon her countenance and wondered why she was unhappy. She continued the song and occasionally wiped away tears before placing the pan in the oven. It was as if she thought, I'm hurting, but I must keep going.

She had several reasons to be sad. Maybe her heart was broken from the death of her parents when she was a young child. Maybe she thought about the abuse of her childhood, the sudden death of her first-born child, or the tragic last hours of my father. Whatever the reason, she was as quiet as she was strong and never expounded on the source of her pain.

However, those sorrows temporarily disappeared during Christmas, her favorite time of the year. She couldn't afford gifts, but she always scraped together funds to purchase a big box of apples and oranges, and small bags of nuts and candies. We always cut a small spruce tree from a nearby field and strung it with homemade decorations such as popcorn strings.

My favorite moment of the season was when she lay me across her lap and sang the words of the classic, Santa Claus is Coming to Town. The sound of her voice was etched in my mind as she softly sang and rocked me to sleep.

As I did with my father at bedtime, I stared at her face and took note of every scar, wrinkle, and blemish. She smiled as she sang, but I could feel the pain of her tumultuous past. Yet, I believe she had joy of the present and hope of a better day. She must have said a hundred times, "The Lord will make a way somehow."

As a child, I didn't realize nor appreciate my mother's tremendous sacrifices until I brought home a school assignment that needed her signature. I had seen her sign my papers before, but this time I focused on what she did.

She took the assignment and slowly read over it. She stumbled with large words because of her eighth-grade education. She carefully placed it on her lap and took the pencil I offered. "Right here?" She asked, pointing to the bottom of the sheet.

"Yea," I responded, "right there."

She carefully positioned the pencil and slowly began to write, in cursive, her signature. She wrote slowly and carefully, as if she was painting a picture. When finished, she examined the letters that formed her name, and upon her satisfaction, handed the paper back to me and smiled.

Her eyes sparkled and her face formed an expression of accomplishment.

I believe she wanted me to be proud of her for writing her name. I was proud of all the difficult sacrifices she made and the education she gave up for her family. But the thing that moved me most were her hands.

Over her lifetime, she went through things no woman should endure. She labored in the fields and dragged large cotton sacks, weighing between 80 and 100 pounds down long rows in sweltering heat. She picked cotton until her fingers bled from the sharp pricks on the cotton bolls. The hoe she used to chop cotton created painful blisters and calluses on her hands. At times, during the short lunch breaks in the field, I sat beside her and watched as she wiped the blood from her hands, wrapped strips of cloth around them, and finished the day despite the pain.

As a runt of a child around four or five years old, I often served as her manicurist by cutting her nails and massaging her hands after a long grueling day in the fields.

"Charlie," she called to me, "get the alcohol and rub my hands."

I grabbed the bottle of rubbing alcohol and a small cloth and sat beside her as she relaxed in her rocking chair.

"Okay, Ma, give me your hand," I said.

She placed one hand in my lap. I poured a little alcohol on the cloth and gently rubbed it over her hand. I could feel her flinch from the sting in her wounds and the pain in her joints. I tried to be as gentle as possible. At those times, I noticed the awful condition of her hands.

They were not the feminine hands of a typical female. They were not smooth, soft, and beautiful. Instead, her hands were rough, heavily scarred, and swelled in the joints from years of untreated arthritis. Her hands were the victims of a lifetime of merciless submissions to the harsh elements of country drudgery.

When I was in my early teens, still rubbing her hands, I realized what those hands had sacrificed for me and my siblings. She never verbalized it, but her actions spoke, "I'm sacrificing for you so your hands will never look like my hands."

It was her hands that managed to raise ten children and keep them fed and clothed even after the tragic death of my father. It was those hands that led me to give my life to Jesus and taught me how to pray. It was those hands that inspired me to finish college—the first in my family. It was those hands that held me tight after my thirteen-year-old son suddenly died from an undetected heart condition.

Although, we laid her to rest after her passing, still, during the difficult times of my life, I can feel the strong embrace and loving compassion of her hands. So, I want to tell my momma in heaven,

> *"Thank you, Momma. Although your hands were destined to pick cotton, you sacrificed so my hands could be destined to pick presidents."*

***

Assimilation Mindset

American history details the forced colonization of North America by European settlers from England, France, Spain, and the Netherlands (Dutch).

Colonization is the forced occupation and takeover of another territory—usually resulting in the dominance of the natives of that land. Colonization was common throughout world history, and this practice was carried out by multiple world military powers. Sometimes, the ruling force allowed the natives to continue practicing their cultures and beliefs. At other times, the ruling force assimilated the natives into their culture, practices, and beliefs.

Colonization Assimilation is when the ruling powers force their cultures, beliefs, and practices upon the indigenous natives and others. This is what happened in North America. European English culture, beliefs, and practices were required by those in authority for natives and Africans to live in American society.

This fact does not mean white European settlers were "evil oppressors" as some have stated. This simply means the European settlers were human and subject to the same character flaws as many past ruling powers—including black ruling powers throughout history.

Sadly, some racial discussions describe slavery and racism as if they were invented by white people. But a careful study of world history proves that belief to be false. It would be worthwhile to read about African Empires and others around the world where slavery and racism were commonplace.

African kingdoms such as the Moors from Northern Africa enslaved white and black people. The Kush dynasty was an ancient kingdom in Nubia centered along the Nile Valley in what is northern Sudan and southern Egypt. These dynasties ruled many years before the transatlantic slave trade, and they practiced slavery and racism as the norm.

They prove that slavery and racism is not a white man's invention, but a human character flaw that affects all races. Here is a link from world history that describes the seven influential African empires as well as a link that discusses the Moors and white slaves.

https://www.history.com/news/7-influential-african-empires
https://www.historynet.com/how-long-did-the-moors-have-white-slaves.htm

Blacks were not Equal in the North nor South

Although many white Europeans in northern states did not want blacks to be enslaved, they also did not want them to be equal with whites, and they supported assimilation of minorities into European culture.

Here are some comments by political leaders about Natives. While some leaders thought highly of them and desired to build an America where both sides could live together in peace, other leaders regarded Natives as uncivilized and in need of assimilation before accepting them into American society.

George Washington: "In 1795, in his Seventh Annual Message to Congress, Washington intimated that if the U.S. government wanted peace with the Indians, then it must give peace to them, and that if the U.S. wanted raids by Indians to stop, then raids by American "frontier inhabitants" must also stop." (Wikipedia)

Thomas Jefferson: "Jefferson initially promoted an American policy that encouraged Native Americans to become assimilated, or "civilized".[29] As president, Jefferson made sustained efforts to win the friendship and cooperation of many Native American tribes, repeatedly articulating his desire for a united nation of both whites and Indians.." (Wikipedia)

Andrew Jackson: "Jackson's involvement in what became known as the Trail of Tears cannot be ignored. In a speech regarding Indian removal, Jackson said, "It will separate the Indians from immediate contact with settlements of whites; free them from the power of the States; enable them to pursue happiness in their own way and under their own rude institutions; will retard the progress of decay, which is lessening their numbers, and perhaps cause them gradually, under the protection of the Government and through the influence of good counsels, to cast off their savage habits and become an interesting, civilized, and Christian community." (Wikipedia)

The implication of Andrew Jackson's comments, and those of many other leaders of his day who held the same opinions, was Non-European cultures, practices, and beliefs of minorities (Natives, Blacks, etc) were not interesting, civilized, or American.

Attempts to create an America where Indians lived side-by-side with Europeans failed largely because most Indians rejected white European assimilation. But most African slaves eventually became fully assimilated into white European culture, practices, and beliefs.

The belief that other races have little to no value unless they have been assimilated is what I refer to as Assimilation Mindset. It was not optional in Colonial America. It was required. Sadly, in many situations today, it is still expected before being considered as an American.

It states: "We white Europeans will not tolerate minorities unless they become fully assimilated by practicing our culture, speaking our language, and converting to our religion. But even then, they will never be equal to whites."

The result of that mindset can be seen throughout the history of America. People and races with little to no value tend to be used and portrayed as the scourge of society—constantly represented in a negative way, and mistreated through a variety of means such as:

The Trail of Tears where Natives were forcefully removed from their homelands and marched west of the Mississippi river.

The Tuskegee Experiment where 600 African American men from Macon County, Alabama were enlisted to partake in a scientific experiment on syphilis.

Henrietta Lacks, a black woman experimented on and treated unsuccessfully for cervical cancer in 1951.

Although many northern whites and abolitionists opposed the enslavement of blacks, many of those same people also opposed the full integration of blacks into their respective societies.

For example, some northern church denominations did not allow blacks to serve as leaders and prohibited side-by-side worship and prayer between whites and blacks.

Even after blacks and some natives assimilated into European culture and the acceptance of Christianity; many whites still did not regard them as equal. They were tolerated and, to some degree, acknowledged as American citizens, but still treated as inferior.

Sadly, even in 2020, the year of perfect vision, there remains too many American citizens with the Assimilation Mindset. To them, America is a melting pot where non-white-Europeans must "melt" or assimilate into the white European version of America. Then, they will be tolerated, but never equal. To them, perhaps subconsciously, the following groups of people are not American:

Africans/People of Color (not colored people)
Muslims
Jews
Chinese
Japanese
Asians
Hispanics and Mexicans
Indians (Native Americans and those from India)
Any Non-European White Person.

To some, America is a white English-speaking Christian nation and all non-conformants are considered foreigners. Their culture, language, and religions are not regarded as American. When these individuals formulate images of America, their images are only associated with white European culture. Their images do not include people from the list above. "After all," they may say, "they are not Americans. They are just foreigners."

Most of the political, religious, and social infighting in America is centered on the struggle to keep the European assimilated version of America. Still some whites are continuing to reject other races, cultures, and religions as worthy of being American. They mentally equate their religious theology with their American citizenship theology. They should be separated.

What is required to be accepted into religious citizenship is belief in one's faith. But what is required to be accepted into American citizenship is belief in the constitution which allows all faiths and those with no faith to be included as citizens.

No one should be forced to convert or assimilate into white European culture and religion to be considered as a true American. I am not a believer in the "all roads lead to God" theory. I am a believer in the American constitution which supports the religious freedom of all faiths to safely exist and freely gather to practice their beliefs without the fear of persecution or attacks.

No one should be told:

"Go back where you came from."
"You don't belong here!"
"You're not an American."
"You have no value unless you assimilate."

Forced assimilation emphatically screams, "My race, culture, and religion are the gold-standard that all people should emulate. Your race, culture, and religion are savage and inferior.

Therefore, you should be forcefully converted and civilized into my culture."

At the heart of forced assimilation is the loathing of another person's race, culture, and religion. It is race-worship and idol worship.

Some people who say such things consider themselves to be Christians. But the Christian faith does not support the forced assimilation mindset. Jesus did not forcefully assimilate sinners into the gospel, nor did he consider the unsaved and different to be people of no value.

On the contrary, in various scriptures, God demonstrates His love and care for all people no matter their race, culture, or religion.

"For God so loved the world that He gave His only begotten son, that whoever believes in Him should not perish, but have everlasting life." (John 3:16)

"And he said to him, "You shall love the Lord your God with all your heart and with all your soul and with all your mind. 38 This is the great and first commandment. 39 And a second is like it: You shall love your neighbor as yourself." (Matthew 22:37-39)

"What do you think? If a man has a hundred sheep, and one of them has gone astray, does he not leave the ninety-nine on the mountains and go in search of the one that went astray? And if he finds it, truly, I say to you, he rejoices over it more than over the ninety-nine that never went astray. So it is not the will of my[a] Father who is in heaven that one of these little ones should perish." (Matthew 18:12-14)

If God and Jesus see everyone as people of value, regardless of their race, culture, and even religious beliefs, why can't some Christians also see every different person in America as people of value deserving of the title American?

The Damage of Forced Assimilation

Unfortunately, there are examples around the world of forced assimilation and the resulting damage it caused. From Canada, to Australia, North America, and beyond.

In Canada, the last Indian residential school closed in 1996. On June 11, 2008, Prime Minister Stephen Harper, on behalf of the Government of Canada, issued a public apology. He acknowledged his nation's role in the forced assimilation of the Aboriginal Peoples. Here is a portion.

> *Mr. Speaker, I stand before you today to offer an apology to former students of Indian Residential Schools. The treatment of children in Indian Residential Schools is a sad chapter in our history. Two primary objectives of the residential schools system were to remove and isolate children from the influence of their home, families, traditions and cultures, and to assimilate into the dominant culture.*
>
> *These objectives were based on the assumption that Aboriginal cultures and spiritual beliefs were inferior and unequal. Indeed, some saw it, as it was infamously said, 'to kill the Indian in the child'. We now recognize that it was wrong to separate children from rich and vibrant cultures and traditions, that have created a void in many lives and communities, and we apologize for having done this.*

> *We now recognize that in separating children from their families, we undermined the ability of many to adequately parent their own children and sowed the seeds for generations to follow. The government of Canada sincerely apologizes and asks the forgiveness of the Aboriginal peoples of this country for failing them so profoundly.*

What a heartfelt and sincere apology from a person in leadership. His words indicate his understanding of the grave harm and in some cases, irreparable damage done to the Natives of Canada. How does a nation give people back their lost culture, family ties, native language, land, and scores of other things taken and soiled by forced assimilation?

Here is a link to an encyclopedia article and a booklet that describes what some students in Canada endured.

https://www.thecanadianencyclopedia.ca/en/article/government-apology-to-former-students-of-indian-residential-schools

https://www.anishinabek.ca/wp-content/uploads/2016/07/An-Overview-of-the-IRS-System-Booklet.pdf

In Australia, a territory that was colonized by Great Britain, a similar process of forced assimilation took place. Here are some excerpts from an online article that explained the process and devastating results:

> *In the first half of the twentieth century, right up until the 1960s, the Australian government sought to create a single, uniform white Australian culture. This was pursued through assimilation policies, which had devastating effects on Indigenous communities.....*

Assimilation policies presumed that Indigenous Australians could enjoy the same standard of living as white Australians if they adopted European customs and beliefs and were absorbed into white society.

https://australianstogether.org.au/discover/australian-history/a-white-australia/?gclid=EAIaIQobChMI-N_iu4XX8gIViKeGCh2TsQseEAAYAiAAEgKcoPD_BwE

In America, according to the National Native American Boarding School Healing Coalition (NABS), a Native-run nonprofit, 15 boarding schools and 73 total schools with federal funding remain open as of 2021.

And according to an abstract written by Rebecca Peterson about the impact of Boarding Schools on Native American families, she writes:

"The Native American boarding schools of the 1800's and early 1900's left a crater in Native American societies. Under the pretense of helping devastated Indian Nations, boarding schools created places of assimilation, forcing children to attend and sometimes resorting to what would now be called kidnapping. Many of these children died from homesickness, working accidents, uncontrolled diseases and ill-planned escape attempts.

Language, culture, and religion were among the absent when the children returned home.

One of the most important of the missing was the parenting skills that were honed over the years by the Native American elders, leaving these children lost because they were raised by complete strangers in historical boarding schools."

https://minds.wisconsin.edu/bitstream/handle/1793/66821/Peterson.pdf?sequence=8&isAllowed=y

The National Native American Boarding School Healing Coalition's website further explains the intention behind boarding schools and the tremendous suffrage of the native children and their families:

> *Between 1869 and the 1960s, hundreds of thousands of Native American children were removed from their homes and families and placed in boarding schools operated by the federal government and the churches...*
>
> *The U.S. Native children that were voluntarily or forcibly removed from their homes, families, and communities during this time were taken to schools far away where they were punished for speaking their native language, banned from acting in any way that might be seen to represent traditional or cultural practices, stripped of traditional clothing, hair and personal belongings and behaviors reflective of their native culture.*
>
> *They suffered physical, sexual, cultural, and spiritual abuse and neglect, and experienced treatment that in many cases constituted torture for speaking their Native languages. Many children never returned home, and their fates have yet to be accounted for by the U.S. government.*

An American General, Brigadier General Richard Henry Pratt, the founder and longtime superintendent of the influential Carlisle Indian Industrial School at Carlisle, Pennsylvania, once said the following about Indian Assimilation:

> *A great general has said that the only good Indian is a dead one, and that high sanction of his destruction has been an enormous factor in promoting Indian massacres. In a sense, I agree with the sentiment, but only in this: that all the Indian there is in the race should be dead. Kill the Indian in him, and save the man.*

https://boardingschoolhealing.org/education/us-indian-boarding-school-history/

Here were some of the common occurrences at some of these boarding schools:
Children were forcefully taken from their parents and families.

Children were forbidden from speaking their native language.

Children were forbidden from wearing their native clothing.

Children were groomed away from their native appearance to look more American.

Children were taught their religion and native culture were evil and un-American. They were force-fed Christianity.

Some children were abused, sexually assaulted, and even murdered.

Yet, all these horrible things that occurred were done under the pretense of "civilizing" the native "immoral savages." But none of these evil things were civil or moral. They were reprehensible, immoral, and un-American.

Forced assimilation, wherever it is carried out around the world, always has the same goal: to produce people who look like the dominate power—people who speak the same language, wear the same clothing, worship the same God, and have the same customs and beliefs. Those who support forced assimilation do not value uniqueness in other human beings.

They do not see differences in languages and cultures as something to learn from or to admire. They are too busy seeing themselves as gods and trying to create a human society fashioned in their own image.

That was the case in Canada, Australia, North America, and around the world.

Forced assimilation is just another form of racism. Unfortunately, racism is as American as apple pie and still practiced by a significant portion of Americans of all colors.

However, I have faith that one day, We the People, will come together, acknowledge true history, turn from our wicked ways, and allow the Lord to heal our land.

But that includes allowing people with non-white-European customs and beliefs to be valued, respected, and equal in citizenship rights of this great country. We must develop an image of America that contains a variety of colors, religions, and cultures, and not become fearful or intimidated by differences.

Until then, let those of us who believe in the value and equality of all mankind, continue to stand on those prophetic words of the Declaration of Independence—that all men (and women) are created equal. Then we will speed up that day when God's children of all colors can live together in peace and harmony—all under that star spangled banner and glorious flag representing America.

Months before writing this book, I stood in the lobby of a small bank. I noticed a Mexican man standing in line in front of me. The next teller line opened has a young Hispanic woman working it. When he walked up to her, they began speaking to each other in Spanish.

As they exchanged pleasant conversation in their native language, I stood there listening and wondering what they were saying. I don't speak Spanish, but their exchanges sounded beautiful, and they both seemed comfortable speaking their native language around others.

I thought, "Now that's what America should be all about. A land where people's native language is not demonized but welcomed, admired, and used whenever appropriate."

Some Americans might say, "This is America! We speak English here!"

Yes, there is a need to speak a common language and have common rules, regulations, and laws for any society to peacefully operate. But that does not mean other languages should be forbidden or demonized. Instead, they should be valued and appreciated. The same goes for a person's native dress, culture, and religion.

Five Self-Evaluation & Discussion

If you know someone who has been assimilated into American culture, how does he/she feel about it?

What are your immediate feelings when someone speaks a different language or wears native clothing?

Do you think people should be allowed to express their native culture in public places or in business environments in an appropriate way? Why or Why not?

What other points would you want to group-discuss in this chapter?

CHAPTER SIX

WHAT MINORITIES WANT

I did not know it at the time, but five days after our huge argument, my son died.

It was Sunday October 14, 2001, and I was the serving as worship leader at church that day. As customary, the worship leader asked everyone to stand in preparation of signing songs of praise. There was never an issue before, but that day, my thirteen-year-old son Torrell, did not want to stand. As everyone stood to their feet, only one person remained seated. My son.

I stared at him with one of those "You better stand right now" grimaces on my face. After a few seconds of hesitation, he slowly stood. As we worshipped and sang praises to God, I peeked at him in between praises and noticed he was not worshipping as he normally did.

He merely stood still, wearing an expression of discontent. I did not know what was going on with him, but at the time, I did not care. I was infuriated by what I called his lack of respect for worship and for me as the worship leader.

When we arrived at home, I verbally laid into him pretty good. I warned him to get his act together and do not ever disrespect God and embarrass me again. I stormed out of his room without noticing the humiliated expression edged on his face or the tears welling up in his eyes. He ran into his bathroom and slammed the door.

Moments later. Bang! Bang! A loud noise came from Torrell's bathroom door.

"What's that noise! I yelled to my wife from another room.

"It is Torrell!" She yelled back. "He's punching the bathroom door! Honey, you got to come get him! Something is wrong!"

I went to his bathroom door and calmly called to him. "Torrell. Son, I need you to open the door, okay?"

I could hear him crying and sobbing. "Come on son. I know something is wrong. Let us talk about it."

He slowly opened the door, and I took him by the hand and escorted him to a couch in the nearby room. He sat next to me with his head down, tears streaming down his face.

I embraced him and held him close as he continued to release tears. "Son, something is bothering you. Can you tell me about it?" I asked.

"No!" He protested. "It is too personal!" He continued to shed tears. After several unsuccessful attempts to get him to share, I decided to try a different approach. I told him about a school experience I had in school with a bully. I told him it happened in front of a gym full of students and was so hurtful and embarrassing that I wanted to die.

"I don't have to say anything then." He murmured as he wiped away tears.

An expression of confusion formed on my face. "What do you mean son?"

"I don't have to say anything because you told it in your story." He said.

"Oh." I responded. "The same thing happened to you?"

He nodded his head and continued to cry. I embraced him, assured him that I loved him, and asked him to forgive me for being insensitive.

"Son, I'm sorry. I should have been more concerned about what you were going through than about what you did. Can you forgive me?"

He nodded his head. He laid his head on my shoulder and continued to cry, and so did I.

I felt lower than a snake's belly. How could I have been so clueless and cold? What Torrell did that day was out of the ordinary for him and I should have immediately asked what was wrong.

I learned that day to ask questions and be more concerned about the person instead of the act. Instead, the awful way I immediately ridiculed him reminds me of something I refer to as the taskmaster response.

I was glad he and I came to peaceful terms and that he forgave me because five days later, on Oct 19th, he died.

The Taskmaster Response

In pre-civil war south, when slavery was abundant, most slave owners hired a taskmaster who ran the work affairs of the slaves. This person usually served as the overseer to make sure the work of the plantation was being done. The slave owner expected the taskmaster to get as much productivity out of the slaves as possible.

That meant no excuses when it came to slave complaints. Even when the slave had a legitimate problem, it was usually dismissed, belittled, or the slave was discredited by being called lazy.

Some taskmasters developed a hardline approach to dealing with the Negro—be tough, don't take any excuses, and never demonstrate any genuine care and concern for the slave. In doing so, the taskmaster demonstrated he saw the Negro slave not as a person that deserved care and concern, but as an object, a tool much like a plow or a horse to be used in accomplishing the work demanded by the Owner.

This taskmaster's mindset did not die when slavery was declared illegal or even after the civil war. That mindset of dealing with the Negro in a harsh and uncaring fashion was passed from person to person and generation to generation. It was used in other areas of American society such as law enforcement, housing, and social society to name a few.

The taskmaster mentality was based on the myths that black people were stronger, more violent, and to some, even without souls. Therefore, one must deal with them in a harsh and aggressive manner while showing no emotional connection or recognizing them as fully human.

I define the taskmaster response as an immediate hardline reaction or response to a person who has a legitimate need. Historically in America, the taskmaster response to minority requests for equality and freedom have been the typical method of communication from too many white Americans for over 400 years.

Harriot Tubman (1822 – 1913): A former slave who helped lead many blacks to freedom was hunted, threatened, and discredited.

Frederick Douglass (1817 – 1895): A former slave turned Abolitionist, orator, and writer was threatened, black-balled, and discredited.

W. E. B. Du Bios (1868 – 1963): Historian, civil rights activist, and one of the founders of NAACP, was threatened, black-balled, and discredited.

The taskmaster response is not limited to whites. Shamefully, I admit this is somewhat how I responded to my son in the opening of this chapter. Although I loved my son and would never equate him to an object, in the heat of that moment I failed to show care and concern for what he was going through. Momentarily, I behaved as if what he did was more important than the bad things he was experiencing.

I failed to ask a simple question that would have demonstrated my deep care and concern for him at that moment:

"Son, what is the problem? Tell me so I can do something to help you."

When some sports players protested for justice and equal rights by kneeling during the national anthem, some people instantly offered a taskmaster response—harsh, cruel, and demonstrating no care or concern for the message of the pro-testers.

Some said it was the wrong time. They rightfully referred to the moment as sacred.

I understand their point of view. I too have ancestors who fought in wars and served in the military. When given an op-portunity to recognize and honor them and the many others who fought and died for American freedom, I stand, place my hand over my heart, and proudly say the words of the national anthem.

But I have a question for those who make such a statement.

When is the right time to yell I can't breathe because of this knee on my neck?

When is the right time to scream they are hanging me?

When is the right time to cry out from unjust beatings?

When is the right time to say I'm being locked up for a crime I did not commit!

When is the right time to call for help while being brutalized?

Sadly, the insinuation from some of a "right time" to protest is simply a delay-tactic used throughout American history.

Martin Luther King Jr. (1929 – 1968): Minister and civil rights leader, was told "It is not the right time!"

Freedom Riders: (1961): A group of black and white civil rights activists who took bus trips through the South to protest segregated bus terminals, were also told, "It is not the right time!"

Selma to Montgomery Marchers (1965): Three protest marches held in Alabama for civil rights, were beaten and told, "It is not the right time!"

And even after the horrendous murder of George Floyd in 2020, the refrain from some continues to be is, "It is not the right time!"

I have a sincere question for everyone who thinks it wasn't the right time:

When is the right time?

We all have things that are sacred and sentimental, and the national anthem is certainly one of them. But when people cry out to us for help, even during the anthem, let us not respond like taskmasters, but like concerned citizens by asking the question, "What is the problem?"

History proves there has never been a right time for many white Americans to discuss racism openly with the intent to make things better.

If you disagree with that statement, here is a challenge. If you can locate a poll taken of white Americans during the past two hundred years, which shows at least 51% of white Americans in favor of openly discussing racism and doing something about it, I will update this book with the poll.

Here is a 2020 article that shares various race poll results among blacks and whites. It clearly shows blacks and whites see the same racial issues very differently.

American Attitudes and Race (gallup.com)

***

What Minorities Want

A black Pastor friend in Georgia shared a shocking incident that happened between himself and a group of white Pastors some time ago. He attended a racial healing event with fellow white Pastors in the area in hopes of bridging the racial divide.

The event was inspiring, and the hosts and attendees were gracious. Toward the end of the event, the host invited him to say a few words. As he approached the microphone, a white Pastor in the audience yelled to him,

"What do ya'll want now?"

Shocked and taken off guard, he managed to pull himself together to deliver a few words of hope and healing. But that Pastor's mentality was on full display for all to see.

I want to take a moment and assume his question was genuine. Perhaps he really wanted to know what blacks and other minorities wanted. Here is a list of wants some minorities shared with me over the years.

Minorities want equality.

In contrast to some messaging on TV and social media that constantly claim, "they are coming to get you" or "they are going to replace you", minorities simply want equality. They want to be seen as equal to everyone else in society. No special privileges or status—just equality.

Minorities want opportunity.

Again, the false messaging that most minorities are welfare recipients or take advantage of working-class people's tax dollars is rampant. Minorities want to prove themselves by working hard and becoming contributors to a strong American society. All they need is opportunity.

Minorities want to be heard.

The taskmaster response is often used toward those minorities who point out racism. Minorities long for the day when the majority of white America will listen and show interest in their pleas.

Minorities want their native customs and cultures to be valued.

We've discussed forced assimilation and the great harm it causes minorities. No one should be forbidden to speak their native language or ostracized for wearing their native clothing or practicing their native religion.

Finally, Minorities want to be loved by the very country they have come to, worked hard for, and fell in love with.

America is a nation where most people confess some type of faith, yet at critical times of racial reconciliation, the display of love is often lacking. Taskmaster responses such as instant verbal attacks, dismissal of a person's legitimate concern, and even physical attacks demonstrate a severe lack of love. It should not be difficult to show basic human concern for others if we truly are who we profess to be.

A black National Basketball Association Coach summed it all up after the horrific killing of George Floyd.

> *"It's amazing why we keep loving this country and this country does not love us back."* Doc Rivers – NBA Coach

✳✳✳

In 1997, my wife and I had a tiny, rambunctious, and extremely curious little girl named Kiana. At age four, she often sampled strange products as part of her diet. She sampled dirt. She sampled hair grease. But her favorite non-edible product was hand lotion. If she did a commercial for breakfast cereal, her tagline would have been, "Hand lotion, the breakfast of Champions."

One day, she was in her room playing with her collection of toys, which included a set of small marbles. I listened from another room as she made loud rambling sounds. Suddenly, the noises stopped. I was curious and went to investigate.

To my horror, I saw my little girl grasping at her throat, struggling to speak. I instantly realized she must have tried to sample one of the small marbles, and it was stuck in her throat. She couldn't breathe!

Frantic, I yelled to my wife, "Call 911! Kiana can't breathe!"

I picked her up and attempted to dislodge the marble, but nothing worked. I was terrified and desperate. I will never forget the expression of fear in my daughter's eyes during those horrific moments. Her eyes spoke to me, even pleaded with me, for help. If she could have spoken, I imagine she would have said, "Daddy, please help me before I die! I can't breathe!"

As my wife explained the situation to the 911 operator, I continued to work feverishly trying to clear her airway. But still nothing. After working on her for a few more seconds that seemed like years, out popped the small marble, and it landed on the carpeted floor.

Kiana instantly took several deep breaths and released them. She cried and so did we. We hugged and kissed her, wiped away her tears and ours, and threw the marble set away. At that moment, nothing was more important or sacred than saving her life.

Kiana's breath was temporarily taken away and her story had a happy ending. However, many minorities have figuratively and literally struggled to breathe and cried out in many ways, "I Can't Breathe!"

Instead of the majority of white America coming to their rescue, many have chosen the taskmaster's response and have even transformed a desperate cry for help into a liberal slogan that strikes fear in the hearts of some whites.

Minorities continue to cry out to Americans and others around the world by asking, "How long?"

My hope and faith both speak to me and declare, "Not Long!"

Six: Self-Evaluation & Discussion

Have you experienced a time when someone you loved was in danger? If you can, please describe how that made you feel?

Do you agree that life itself is sacred and valuable? Why or Why not?

Which minority want do you agree with and are there other wants not listed in the book?

What other points would you want to group-discuss in this chapter?

CHAPTER SEVEN

RACIAL COMMUNICATION

D uring the 1950s and 1960s, my family lived in several locations throughout the county—mainly in small houses owned by white landowners. This wasn't uncommon for families of sharecropper farmers. Usually, the homeowner and sharecropper worked out a deal for the family to remain if sharecropping continued.

My family was accustomed to constant relocation. We usually had advance notice before the home had to be vacated. Of course, there were times when things didn't work out so smoothly. One of those times occurred in the middle of winter. Several inches of snow blanketed the frozen ground. As midday approached, snow continued to float down from the sky like feathers riding on the wind.

My father, John, rested in his favorite chair, casually smoking his pipe. My mother, Pearl, rocked in her rocking chair as she put the finishing touches on a quilt sewn from patches of old clothes. The children sat by the small fireplace—trading stories of the day and soaking in all the warmth they could muster when suddenly a loud noise came from the front door. "Bang, bang, bang!"

The children stopped talking. All eyes in the room went toward the door. John and Pearl glanced at each other. "Who could that be on a day like this?" John asked.

The banging continued and the force shook the tiny house. "Bang, bang, bang!"

John rose from his chair, laid down his pipe, moved toward the door, and yelled out, "Who's knocking?"

"It's me!" The landlord yelled. "Open the door!"

John opened the door and found himself face-to-face with an agitated white landlord. He delivered the news bluntly. "Y'all need to get yo stuff together and find yourself another house!"

John's face revealed the total shock and dismay he must have felt. He managed to form a few words. "But you said we could stay here till winter was up and see about cropping for you next year...."

"I know what I said!" The landlord sharply interrupted. "That fool son of mine done went off and got himself married, and they don't have a place to stay. They ain't staying in my house, so y'all got to move. I'm gone give this house to them."

Apparently still reeling from the shock of the moment, John offered a reluctant, "Okay."

Then came the obvious question from John. "When we got to be gone? How much time you gon' give us?"

The landlord looked John in the eyes. "Now!" He coldly responded. "Y'all need to get yo stuff together and leave as soon as y'all can."

John looked him in the eyes. "Where the hell we gon go in this weather?"

The landlord slowly turned to walk away, then looked back to offer a final word. "That ain't my problem."

He briskly walked away and disappeared into the snowy day.

John slowly closed the door. He leaned his head against the wooden frame and pounded it with his fist. "Damn!" He yelled.

He slowly turned to face his family and looked at the dazed faces of his children and the worried face of his wife.

"I'll pack our things and get the kids ready," Pearl said.

"I'll get the wagon and mule hitched." John slowly conceded.

He put on a few layers of clothing and went outside to prepare the wagon. Pearl called to the children, "y'all come here."

They gathered around her rocking chair. "Now, y'all need to put on some more clothes, two pairs of socks, and a few shirts. I want y'all to be warm while we are riding in the cold."

"But where we going?" One of the older kids chimed in.

She responded, "We will know when we get there, baby. Now you just do what I say."

They each went their own way following Pearl's instructions as she gathered their meager belongings in handmade sacks. John pulled the wagon around and threw the sacks and other belongings in the wagon.

Pearl carefully loaded the children in the back among the sacks and small pieces of furniture—stuffing any opening between them with clothing and quilts. The children, unaware of the peril the family faced, seemed to enjoy the event as they reached out to catch drifting snowflakes.

John and Pearl climbed into the front of the wagon—wiping snowflakes from their eyes. Pearl snuggled close to John—adjusting the side flaps on his hat to cover his ears. "Which way we gon go?" She asked.

He carefully surveyed the possibilities and finally responded, "We go north to another farm. I think they might have a house there."

He looked at her, and she offered him a smile to help ease his frustration and deep concern. He snapped the reins and yelled the move-out command, "Giddyap, mule!"

The wagon wheels parted the deep snow—leaving only a temporary trail as they pulled out in search of a home.

***

Racial Communication

Effective communication is key to resolving racial tension and conflict. To forge racial unity, we must voluntarily enter open and frank dialogue that ultimately fosters increased understanding and mutual respect.

This first step can be the most difficult given the current toxic climate of hatred and misinformation. Also, most people prefer to avoid challenging discussions—thinking it best to keep silent and peaceful rather than confront and overcome.

Too often, the unsuccessful communication path of:

Passion ☐ Verbal Attack ☐ Silence ☐Separation is followed by heated conversations. This only leads to further alienation and increased racial conflict. Instead, the successful path of Passion ☐ Communication ☐ Listening ☐ Understanding should be used to reduce conflict and encourage unity.

There are two things people tend to seek in heated confrontations that lead to communication break downs:

Agreement vs. Understanding

Most people tend to want others to agree with their point of view and often fight hard to hear a person say, "I agree with you."

But that will rarely happen—especially in heated debates. Some people can forcefully push their points that make total sense to them and become frustrated when others don't bow and give in. That often leads to verbal attacks, criticism, and even expulsion of the person from the conversation. The result is often mental, emotional, and conversational separation.

Instead, people should first seek a personal understanding of another's point of view and how they arrived at that belief or opinion. Secondly, share experiences and opinions in a compassionate but respectful manner to help others understand, not necessarily agree.

Give good explanations, examples, and make connections with the experiences of others while giving people room to express their point of view. This requires patience, humility, and wisdom with words. Perhaps this is the reason there tends to be more racial separation than racial unification.

Equal Emphasis vs. Leeway

People are different in many ways—culture, experience, and race are just a few. Given this fact, it is natural for different individuals to place different emphases on certain aspects of race related topics.

One person may emphasize the phrase Black Lives Matter more than the phrase All Lives Matter, indicating black lives should be seen with the same value as other lives. Another may reverse the phrases with the justification that all lives should matter with the same degree of importance.

Giving others leeway to express themselves without demanding lockstep agreement on things like the order of words and phrases can create an open atmosphere of communication where all feel comfortable to contribute without retribution.

$$***$$

Styles of Communication

People have different styles of communicating. Some of these styles include:

Detailed vs. Summary

Some people are incredibly detailed and tend to share the smallest occurrences even if those occurrences don't apply to the subject matter. They tend to be longwinded and can lose listeners as a result.

Others tend to summarize their thoughts and opinions in a few words—leaving plenty of room for listener curiosity and interpretation. This can lead to confusion and misunderstandings.

Expressive vs. Nonchalant

Some people are extremely expressive and communicate with their entire bodies. Their hands, heads, and body movements all work together when they talk. This can give the impression of anger when they are simply sharing thoughts.

Others tend to be nonchalant—laid back and calm with little body movement or voice inflection—leading listeners to the inaccurate impression that they do not care. They may be deeply passionate about the subject matter and may even be upset, but their body language will not indicate their true emotions.

Direct vs. Indirect

Some people are direct and get straight to the point of the subject matter. They do not take the time to build a case. They emphatically state the conclusion and take their seats because they may not be interested in explaining how they arrived at their main point. They can seem insensitive and even callous, but that is not their intention.

Others can be indirect and take a considerable amount of time laying the foundation for a case before delivering a conclusion. They may present reasons and explanations first and eventually deliver the conclusion a long time afterwards.

Absolute vs. Balanced

Some people are absolute thinkers and tend to converse in resolute or general terms by putting all people into one group, even though some may not belong to that group. They tend to use all-inclusive language such as them and us—mentally building stereotypes so they can easily associate them with their frame of mind.

Others are balanced and realize all people in any group are not the same. They tend to use selective language such as some people because they want to be accurate.

Which of these styles do you use when communicating? Can you determine which styles are more likely to result in disagreement and which styles could clash even to the point of violence? It would be good to recognize your communication style as well as the styles of others. Knowing this could help navigate around the rough spots of an interaction.

Tools of Effective Communication

Successful communication is rarely accidental. It is usually intentional—utilizing tools of effective communication—especially during potentially heated interactions. Here are some tools of effective communication:

The Three Do Nots: JEP—Justify, Excuse, Pivot

There are three things one should not do when discussing racism or any other hot-button topic.

One, do not Justify slavery and racism. For example. Some people may say, "Slavery made you better off because you were civilized and taught Christianity."

This is a common tactic people use to refuse to admit any wrongdoing. Instead, they suggest all the hurt of the bondage was somehow for the slaves' good—even hinting slave owners were fulfilling God's divine order. In so doing, they fail to consider the thousands of blacks who died on the slave routes from inner Africa to the shoreline. They ignore the desperation of the Africans who jumped overboard or died in the filthy slave ship conditions. Those who died did not get the chance to be civilized or converted.

Two, do not Excuse clear evidence. For example, some people deny the overwhelming evidence of systemic and institutional racism. They chose to accept the common excuse that all racial incidents are isolated instead of many being coordinated and organized.

And three, do not Pivot. An example of pivoting is when a person says, "Yes, but what about black-on-black crime, single parent households, and high school dropout rates that affect blacks?"

Pivoting is an indication that the person does not want to face tough questions, so he or she redirects the conversation to some equally distasteful reality. In the case of racism, many pivot on the question of their ancestors' historical role in slavery and oppression. It is human nature to deflect, which is a form of pivoting, when one has become uncomfortable and perhaps unprepared.

The best way to successfully discuss racism and other passionate and important subject matters is to be open, honest, and humble. For example, admit you may not understand certain aspects of racism and have not experienced some discriminations, but will attempt to ask and answer the tough questions to the best of your ability.

Mental Posture

Defense is natural when engaging in controversial talks. People often feel the need to defend their stance, belief, or race. But this mental posture only fuels the conflict because those who are out to defend are not out to understand—only to respond with rebuttals and comebacks.

That defensive posture needs to change to a posture of understanding. That means not seeking to form an immediate response but allowing time to really think about the information shared.

Pause, think, and ask key questions to make sure you understand the speaker's position and point. It may be necessary at times to share what you believe the speaker is saying for clarification.

This will alleviate misunderstandings that lead to conflict. Franklin R. Covey said, "Seek first to understand, then to be understood."

Sometimes, people can also adopt a posture of proof—setting out to prove that their beliefs and opinions are the right ones instead of an alternate one. This can also cause the dismissal of other points of views and opinions.

The answer is to adopt a posture of reconciliation instead of a posture of proof. There are times when a person's solution is to simply offer an alternate solution. Once the point has been clearly made, it should be left up to the listener to accept or reject the solution.

De-Escalation

There will be times when the interplay of passionate conversation will lead to tense exchanges. When that happens, it will be necessary to perform de-escalation techniques. One such technique is to simply smile. A smile tends to make others calm and demonstrates the smiler is not upset. A smile can immediately reduce contention, so it should be used often.

Another technique is to take a timeout or a pause to allow all parties to breathe and collect their thoughts. A 30-second or one-minute period of silence and deep breathing can be a welcome interruption to difficult conversations. It allows each party to regroup, and return prepare to reattempt meaningful dialogue.

A third technique is to disagree respectfully—usually by starting with a compliment and following it with a carefully worded response that does not criticize the person but shows the flaw in the person's belief or opinion. For example, "I respect your passion about this subject matter, but I would like to offer an alternative point of view."

Most people will consider an opposing opinion if it is presented in a respectful manner

Listening

Growth only happens in a tough conversation with careful listening. But that takes an overwhelming desire to want to know someone's experiences and opinions. Self-expression is self-gratifying but listening to others allows you to connect with others. They are disarmed by your willingness to allow them to express themselves.

But there is an art to listening; the barriers to effective listening need to be removed. The first barrier is preconceived notions. All people have a certain degree of prejudice and bias which affects how they interpret information from others.

For example, when talking to a person from the opposite political party, some may interpret all things the speaker says as an attack on his or her party. The same can happen in racism discussions.

When blacks and whites have intense racial conversations, it can be easy to misunderstand or accuse each other of making racially insensitive statements. The speaker should be given the benefit of the doubt when information is questionable. Sometimes simply asking someone to repeat a phrase or statement will clear up confusion. At other times, it may be necessary to ask for further clarification or explanations with examples.

It is always best to make sure you have an accurate understanding before responding to or criticizing a person's point of view. That way, the conversation can stay on the right track even if it ends with the agreement to disagree.

With effective communication, hot-button topics such as racism can be mastered and giant strides toward much-needed racial reconciliation can be achieved.

Entering the Racial Conversation

> *"Examine yourselves, to see whether you are in the faith. Test yourselves. Or do you not realize this about yourselves that Jesus Christ is in you? —unless indeed you fail to meet the test!" (2 Corinthians 13:5,2 Peter 1:10-11)*

The reason we should discuss racism, from slavery to now, is to come to terms with the truth of the past and examine what mindsets, beliefs, and practices led to one of the most shameful periods in U. S. history: the slave trade and Civil War.

Then, identify the wrongs such as supremacy and racism, and examine ourselves to see it any of those destructive beliefs are operating in our lives.

As African Americans, we should humbly enter the conversion as if we too could harbor the same beliefs and practices they did in the past, and not assume white people could never identify with the humiliating feeling of racism. We must believe they can contribute to the conversation and that we have room to learn and grow.

If everyone humbled themselves and entered the conversation understanding that he or she may have traces of those destructive mindsets, then racism will be properly addressed, the divide healed, and the Nation led into racial peace.

Race Communication Tip #1: Acknowledge Human Color

I get the phrase, "When I look at you, I don't see color." It is an attempt at suggesting the speaker is not racist. It is intended as a compliment, but in reality, it is an insult.

If a person can marvel at the beautiful colors of a bouquet of flowers, a rainbow sitting above an ocean, and a breathtaking sunrise or sunset, how is it possible to look at the remarkable colors of humans and become colorblind? We should never pretend not to see the beauty of the many shades of skin we encounter daily. Let us open our eyes and extend our love for nature's colors to the love of human beings.

Race Communication Tip #2: Acknowledge Human Difference

One person asked, "Why are we teaching our children that skin color makes them different?" The short answer: "Because it does make them different."

A person's skin color is one aspect of what defines that person's appearance. So it should not be discounted or ignored. Instead, it should be acknowledged and celebrated. In the past and in some cases today, a person's skin color was used either as a pass for privilege or a scarlet letter for a doomed life. But skin color does not make people different in a bad way, it makes them different in a good way.

We must change the way we talk about race. We must talk about it in a positive way.

Beware of Race Projection

As a young teenager in the 1970s, coming off the heels of a violent and turbulent civil rights movement in America, I often listened to militant civil rights leaders and groups. One of my favorites was Malcom X, a Black Muslim civil rights leader who believed in using violence if needed to combat racism.

He said such things as:

"Free yourself by any means necessary!"

"We didn't land on Plymouth Rock, my brothers and sisters—Plymouth Rock landed on us."

"Be peaceful, be courteous, obey the law, respect everyone; but if someone puts his hand on you, send him to the cemetery."

"Nobody can give you freedom. Nobody can give you equality or justice or anything. If you're a man, you take it."

As a young black man struggling with self-image and trying to find black dignity in the world around me, I ingested many of the militant thought patterns about black victimization. Beliefs such as:

A black person must be twice as smart as a white person to be given a fair chance.

A black person must be twice as talented as a white person to be considered equal.

A black person cannot get ahead in life without being plotted against by "the man" (the white power structure).

Unfortunately, the world I lived in and the immediate people around me did very little to counter these mindsets. As a young black man, I often experienced being closely followed in stores, asked more questions by business owners than white counterparts, and the piercing uneasy stares of some white people in certain situations.

As a result, I projected or cast racist mindsets and attitudes onto some white people who were not racist. I thought their communication and actions were always motivated by black hatred. Thus, my response to their everyday interaction and conversation was that of defensiveness and their actions were always suspect.

Race projection is something I have struggled with for many years. For example, months before writing this book, I was in a grocery store using the self-checkout line. The area was packed with people using checkout terminals. When one terminal opened, I carried my basket of items and began to scan.

A few moments later, the young white store clerk who worked the self-checkout area walked over close to me and stood there watching me as I scanned my items.

I casually looked around the checkout area and noticed all other people checking out were white. I wondered, "Why did the clerk choose to stand beside ME, of all the people, and watch over? I can pay for my stuff! The nerve of him!"

These and other unpleasant thoughts about the clerk ran through my head. I wanted to ask him, "Why did you stand beside me? Do you think I will steal something by not scanning it?"

As I scanned items, I looked at him and smiled. "Hi young man." I said. "How are you today?"

"Fine Sir." He replied with a smile.

There were a few seconds of awkwardness and I believe he read the curiosity on my face.

"Sir," he said with the same smile. "I'm standing here because I saw you had coupons and I will need to enter my code before you can finish your checkout."

"Oh." I said with a hint of surprise. I glanced at the coupons in my hand, looked at him, and smiled.

"Thank you young man." I whispered. "That is very thoughtful."

I took my bags and walked out breathing a huge sigh of relief and being thankful I did not follow my instinct and accuse that wonderful young man of being a racist.

I had, in my mind, projected or cast a racist attitude upon him simply by his action of standing close to me during checkout. Can you understand why I felt that way? But even understanding why does not make it okay. It is clearly a mental hurdle that I still need to overcome.

Race projection works in all directions. Blacks can project racist attitudes onto whites. Whites can project militant attitudes onto blacks. All races can do it to anyone of another race and it is a major hurdle to overcome in the struggle for racial healing.

In fact, some people can say racist things but not actually be racist. How is that possible? Some people can lash out in anger or pain and seek to use the worse words possible to hurt others. They don't possess the racist beliefs of supremacy or separation. But in the heat of frustration words can be used as weapons.

Over the course of my life, I have certainly used words as weapons and have uttered things I longed to take back. I really did not mean what I said. I just wanted that person to hurt.

Therefore, please be careful about branding someone a racist solely because of what he or she says. Find out more about that person before. Perhaps he or she may be hurting and merely trying to place hurt on others.

Have you ever done something similar? Have you assumed something someone of another race did or said was racist without knowing all the facts? If so, could it have been a case of race projection?

As mentioned previously in this book, we cannot change others, but we can change ourselves. One of the goals of this book to get you, the reader, to perform a serious self-examination of your thoughts, motivations, and actions.

Is there anything about your thinking that should be re-evaluated or changed?

Seven: Self-Evaluation & Discussion

Which communication styles do you use?

Have you done or witnessed someone do the JEP (Justify, Explain away, or Pivot) while talking about race?

Are you comfortable talking about race with people in other race groups? Why or Why not?

What other points would you want to group-discuss in this chapter?

CHAPTER EIGHT

RACIAL UNITY

A white guy with a rebel flag exposed my bias as a black man. He was my coworker in the early 1980s—a weird character who stood at six feet two inches with a bushy beard. He looked like a typical hardline biker. After months of observation, I realized he was a big man with a big heart. He helped anyone in need. We became good friends and often talked, laughed, and joked around.

He invited me to lunch one day and offered to drive. When we walked outside, I immediately noticed the huge rebel flag draped across the back window of his ford truck. I hesitated, pointed to the flag, and said, "Dude, what is that?"

Surprised, he asked, "What do you mean?"

As we rode to lunch, I took the time to explain what the rebel flag meant to me which was over 400 years of suffering for blacks. He listened and seemed to take in what I was saying, but still insisted the flag represented his heritage, not hatred.

Over the next few weeks, we had several conversations about the flag. Some were intense and almost argumentative. But he said something one day that made me think. "Charlie, I know what the flag means to you, but can I explain what it means to me?"

I agreed to listen.

He continued, "Some of my people use this flag to keep hatred alive and somehow revive the Civil War. But I use it to honor my ancestors who fought for what they believed was their way of life. I realize portions of their way of life was wrong. Owning slaves and mistreating others was wrong, and I regret that part of their lives.

But that's not all they were about. Everyone's ancestors did some wrong things—including your ancestors. I hope the way I treat you shows who I am and what I believe."

I thought long and hard about his words and eventually realized he was right. He had exposed a racial bias in me. I thought ALL people who carried or honored the rebel flag were racists. But I had come to know him and discovered he was nowhere near the racist category.

I finally realized there is something called, "the totality of a person." Meaning a person should not be judged based on one aspect of his or her life. My coworker's message was,

"Yes, they had racial issues, but race alone should not define who they were as people. They were parents, siblings, community leaders, and much more. I condemn their wrong racial beliefs, but I honor their totality as my ancestors."

I somewhat understood his point of view. I thought about my family and the several "crazy uncles" I had to contend with every family reunion. They were people who had good hearts and would do anything for anyone in the family. But they had issues in certain areas of their thinking, including racial areas.

In terms of human totality, they were not bad people, but they did have issues.

He did not change my mind about the rebel flag. I will always see it as a negative representation of the struggles of my people. But he did change my mind about people. Now, I realize not everyone who waves the rebel flag is a racist.

As a result of our intense and deep conversations, we grew even closer as friends. A strange thing happened when I rode in his truck with the huge rebel flag. The flag seemed to fade into the background. We talked, laughed, and joked—even in that truck with the rebel flag.

I grew from those discussions and realized true maturity is reflected in our decision to love and respect others regardless of disagreements.

Racial Unity

After the death of George Floyd while in the custody of white officers, a racial rainbow of people flooded the streets—joining blacks in their fight against police brutality and equality. They carried signs, lifted their voices, and sang in unison the words "We Shall Overcome." The horrific eight minutes and forty-six seconds of torture were recorded and broadcasted around the world, and the world responded in an unprecedented fashion. Thousands swept through the cities, suburbs, and even rural areas to send a resounding message of No More!

The time was right, and their massive presence was beautiful to see. There is beauty in real unity—when diverse people come together with a common message to fight for a common agenda. All races must unify if we are going to triumph in this difficult fight for equality. Here are some areas where we need to unite.

Unite our Voices

Say his name! George Floyd! That was the powerful chant and refrain during protests and marches around the world. Those words unified thousands in America and globally in nations around the world. When they shouted his name, their strength seemed to increase with each repetition. Their voices were heard for miles as their presence overwhelmed towns and cities.

As a result of their powerful determination, local and state leaders began to change policies and procedures as they also began to enact laws to address police reform. But that much-needed change was only the beginning.

The power of unified voices carries weight with officials. Marches and protests have proven to be effective at driving needed change. But these actions should remain peaceful and law-abiding if they are going to be effective at ushering in reform.

Therefore, keep marching, protesting, and demonstrating peacefully and continue to abide by all laws so efforts can be instrumental in enacting positive change.

Unite in Truth

Supremacy and Racism are passed on from generation to generation through lies and misinformation. Today, with the many avenues of information, truth can be very hard to identify. Social media, podcasts, talk shows, and television seem to be slanted in one direction.

But all races should unite around the truth about America's challenging history, the complex present, and the hopeful future. All Americans must continue to tell the true story of the American civil war and correct the twisted notion that those times were somehow great.

All people should unite to face the continued racial disparities that still exist today in the areas of employment, healthcare, housing, and others. We must collectively identify the policies, procedures, and laws that allow discrimination and push hard for change. This means we need to become familiar with the various reports and the data on which they are built. Someone once said, "Data don't lie, but people do."

Unite in Justice

Martin Luther King, Jr. once said, "Injustice anywhere is a threat to justice everywhere."

Injustice is the result of a lack of accountability and correction in our judicial system.

African Americans are not strangers to gross injustice. From slavery to civil war, to reconstruction, and to the civil rights era and beyond, blacks have historically been targets of systemic acts of injustice. Slave owners had complete authority to brutalize and even kill slaves with no accountability or correction.

Post-Civil War and into reconstruction period those same acts continued against freed blacks who were attempting to find their place in society. They were often met with beatings, terrorism, and lynching with no accountability. In fact, at times the local law enforcement were the ones who carried out the attacks or knew the perpetrators and did nothing.

Unfortunately, that system of injustice has survived and found its way into our modern system of law enforcement. I am convinced most officers are good men and women who strive for excellence in performing their duties.

But there are some officers who join for all the wrong reasons, constantly break rules, and seek shortcuts all to the detriment of the department. These bad officers believe they can do whatever they want to whomever they want, without consequences. And sadly, most of the time their evil acts go unpunished.

It was astonishing to see, on camera, the smug attitude of the officer who killed George Floyd. As he pressed his knee on Floyd's neck, at times, he looked directly into the camera held by a bystander knowing full well his actions were being recorded. His hands were in his pockets as George Floyd pleaded for his life and constantly said, "I can't breathe."

The officer's facial expression was that of a casual person who did not think what he was doing would bring consequences. Sadly, if his act had not been caught on camera, it probably would not have led to his arrest.

We must continue to unite on equal justice issues and continue to push for law enforcement reform so all races can experience equal justice under the law.

Unite in Access

There are two major roadblocks that hinder access to critical resources: Poverty and discriminatory practices. It is no secret that the poorest people tend to have little to no access to valuable resources such as healthcare, high wage jobs, good education, and good homes in low crime neighborhoods.

In a capitalist society, the institutions require the financial ability to pay; those without the finances are often left behind or are forced to be homeless and fend for themselves. One of the answers to this problem is opportunity. When the poor have opportunities to attend good schools and secure a great education, they are more likely to get high paying jobs and have access to critical resources.

Hindrances to access can also include failure to disclose needed information about resources to minorities—reserving the best resources for whites. Some real estate agents practice this—in effect, creating and protecting white neighborhoods from the presence of minorities.

What can be done about these things? Stand up. Speak out. Unite your voice in opposition to injustice anywhere and everywhere. Whether in written form or practice, barriers to access should be torn down. When all people unite to combat poverty and discrimination, they will create a world where all races of people can fulfill their hopes and dreams.

Unite in Power

Supremacists and racists know the importance of political power. America is a nation of laws, and those who control the formation of policies can use them to create systemic racism. By law, they can determine who gets access to resources and services, who gets financial aid and how much, who goes to which schools, and who gets access to critical care. In some cases, these laws can determine who stays poor and who becomes rich, who dies and who lives, and who fails and who succeeds.

Supremacists fight to gain and keep political control to use it to dominate and control other races. After the Civil War, they were embedded in the Democratic Party until blacks began to come into the party in the 1960s. After slowly leaving the party, they formed third parties in a failed attempt to gain political power.

Many supremacy groups have slowly migrated into politics—taking their views of supremacy and racism which they secretly incorporate into polices and laws. It should be in the best interest of all non-racist party members to strongly oppose them and their policies. (There are racist people in all parties. If you research supremacy groups, you can find their party of choice.)

It is important for good people to occupy seats of political power. America needs leaders who serve the people, not their parties. America needs politicians with the will and courage to call out racism and discriminatory policies and practices wherever they exist.

There should be diversity in power. All races need to be adequately represented at the table when making important policies and laws. Balanced representation can prevent laws that disproportionately affect certain races and classes of individuals. Representation will ensure the needs of people in all races are addressed.

As you examine your local, state, and federal political leaders, do you see enough diversity or are most of your leaders of one race? Is there adequate representation for those who may be marginalized?

Some years ago, my big brother and I became embroiled in a political argument. We were both Democrats, but we disagreed on what to do with political power. I asked, "Why should democrats take control of political power and do the same wrong things Republicans do?"

He thought for a few seconds and responded, "We need to take power just to have it and be the ones in control!"

I pointed out that if that's the only reason to have power, we would just do the same ungodly things to keep it—including develop discriminatory laws to keep other people subdued.

With great power comes great responsibility and those in power should do right by all people, not use it for unfair advantages.

When we unite in all these areas, justice and equality will flow down like a mighty stream upon the heads of all God's children. Then, we can truly live in peace and love as we admonish float down from the sky like feathers riding on the wind.

Eight: Self-Evaluation & Discussion

In my story about my coworker and the rebel flag, how would you have handled that situation?

What are some of the barriers to truly uniting on racial justice and how can those barriers be taken down?

Do you think power (political, financial, or social) plays a big part in the lack of racial unification?

What other points would you want to group-discuss in this chapter?

CHAPTER NINE

RACIAL HEALING

O ften, racism is discussed from a white-against-black point of view. In this section, I want to acknowledge that racism can occur in other ways. It's also committed by some blacks and others. No race is immune to the evils of blatant and covert racism. People are perceived to be racist based on their words or actions. Perception is the way humans view people and situations. It is the complex process of how the human mind evaluates and processes information to arrive at a conclusion that's commonly called an opinion. Human perception is not synonymous with truth. However, most people view their perception as truth.

For example, in a previous chapter, I shared a personal story about a white landlord evicting my family without advanced notice. Most people, especially African Americans, would view the landlord as racist because of his words and actions. I disagree with that perception and opinion.

I believe the landlord would have done the same thing to any family occupying the house at that time—even a white family. He was coldhearted, uncaring, and unsympathetic, but even these things don't make him a racist. The motive the landlord gave for wanting my family to vacate the house was understandable, but it was no reason for him to handle the situation in such a callous manner. I believe he acted out of frustration with his personal situation and in turn mishandled things with my family. I don't believe he did it because my family was black. I believe he did it simply because my family was occupying the house at that time.

My rationale for this conclusion is two-fold. The landlord had two problems and only one solution. His son had a sudden marriage, and they had no place to live. The only solution for him was to find his son a house. He only had one house—the one my family lived in. It would be easy for me to take it a step further in my perception and pretend to know the deepest thoughts and beliefs of the landlord toward race. I could say he was a racist based on my perception, but my perception isn't truth. No one knows the deepest thoughts and beliefs of anyone else unless the person is specifically told or has overwhelming evidence of those thoughts and beliefs.

My point is this: there are times when blacks are treated unfairly, unjustly, and unequally, but not all these incidents are due to racism. I'm not naive—systemic racism is still very much alive and well. However, not every bad incident that happens to blacks at the hands of whites is due to racism. Sometimes people make the wrong decisions and handle tough situations in the wrong manner.

Take the following incidents that happened to me and decide if they were racism.

Incident #1

When I was much younger, I was into weightlifting. I was muscular and bald. Several white and black friends said my normal facial expression was intimidating. One day, I finished another grueling workout and decided to stop by the grocery store. I was wearing a T-shirt that revealed my muscular build, sporting my bald head, and wearing a pair of sunglasses.

As I walked down one aisle, I saw an elderly Caucasian woman standing beside her basket. She had her purse resting on her shoulder as she peered at some items. As I approached her, searching for some items of my own, I noticed she first stared at me as if she was frightened. She clutched her purse closer to her body. After I walked by, I noticed she relaxed her grip on her purse.

My first thought was, I can't believe this woman did that. What is her problem?

Would you say she was a racist?

Incident #2

Years after the prior incident, I developed a completely different look—a corporate image. I lost some of the muscle, grew my hair back, and shaved my face for a clean, professional appearance. One day, I arrived at work early in the morning and had to take the elevator from the parking deck on the roof down to the first floor.

I was neatly dressed wearing a suit and tie, carrying a briefcase, and properly displayed my employee badge on the front of my suit.

I was the only person on the elevator when I boarded it at the roof level. When the elevator stopped at the third floor, the door opened, and there stood a middle-aged Caucasian woman.

She looked at me and jumped as if she was startled. I smiled, turned to face her so she could plainly see my badge, and greeted her with a calming, "Good morning. How are you today?"

She cracked a small smile and seemingly reluctantly walked into the elevator and plastered herself against the farthest wall away from me. I made small talk on the way down, trying to ease her fears.

Would you say she was a racist?

In both cases, I don't believe either woman was a racist. I believe they were people who reacted to the situation: the first woman reacted to a young muscular male wearing sunglasses with a mean look on his face. The second woman reacted to a stranger in an elevator.

I could jump to the conclusion they both behaved in such ways because I was black, but I don't know they would have behaved differently if I were white. Their behavior, in my opinion, was totally unnecessary. I certainly wasn't going to take the woman's purse in the store nor harm the woman in the elevator.

I was deeply offended by their actions, but I've learned not to view my perception as truth. Truthfully, I didn't know either of them and had no way of knowing if their actions were motivated by racism or if they were simply reacting to their own bias fears.

When a person's motivation isn't clear, I've learned to give that person the benefit of the doubt. I believe race relationships will improve as more people learn to adopt this practice.

✳✳✳

Racial Healing

On April 9th, 1865, the four-year American Civil War that divided a nation came to an end. The North won and the Southern General, Robert E. Lee, surrendered to Northern Union General Ulysses S. Grant in the state of Virginia.

The war was officially over, but the bitter issues, including slavery that divided the nation were far from resolved. Lawfully, America put aside the legality of slavery with the Emancipation Proclamation and the thirteenth amendment, but many southern ex-slaveowners did not experience a change of heart regarding their views of racial supremacy. Although the country was reunited on paper, North and South were not together in terms of ideals and principles.

Unfortunately, many southerners continued to harbor supremacist and racist beliefs and simply developed new methods of discrimination against the newly freed slaves. Practices such as the peonage system, Black Codes, and Jim Crow laws started after the Civil War. Other practices such as voter suppression, lynching, and terrorizing of blacks by individuals and groups such as the Klu Klux Klan, became all too common.

However, racism was not limited to southern states and was also embraced by some in the Northern states. This became evident as free blacks began to migrate North to escape southern racism and to seek safety and job opportunities.

In some cases, blacks were met by resistance from northern whites and even attacked. Some whites were fearful that blacks would take scarce employment opportunities. Therefore, racism was not and is not geographical. It was a sickness that spread throughout America and extended from the South to the North, East, and West.

America may have been territorially reunited after the civil war, but the nation is not truly unified in terms of racial philosophy. The country continues to suffer from a dual-brain racial theology where one side believes all races are equal and the other side insists one race is superior to all others.

The centuries old ideologies of supremacy and racism continue to be alive and well—creating an invisible and continued North vs. South battle in politics, principles, and practices.

So how should the nation address healing? Is it possible for a four-hundred-year-old wound to finally mend completely? What will it take for true peace and harmony among blacks and whites? These questions are answered in the following sections.

✳✳✳

Achieving Racial Healing

Confession

Think about the worse, most embarrassing, and immoral thing that ever happened to you. Odds are very few people know about it. Perhaps you hide it in the far corners of your memory and never wanted to discuss it. You probably long to forget it, if you could, and you certainly would not want to create a physical reminder of it and place it on public display for the world to see. In other words, you would not be proud of it and you would not glamorize that shameful thing, even though it was a part of your history. In fact, dwelling on it may even make you emotionally sick.

Part of healing is letting go of the things that make a nation emotionally sick. It seems there are far too many in America who fight to hold on to the symbols of supremacy and racism—including glamorizing the very history of sin they represent. I believe history should serve as a source of learning, but the disgraceful portions of history should never be presented as good nor should they be referenced as great.

For example, years ago a white U. S. Senatorial Candidate for the State of Alabama, and former Alabama Chief Justice, held a rally. A black person asked him when he thought America was last great. He replied by referencing the period of slavery:

> *I think it was great at the time when families were united—even though we had slavery—they cared for one another. Our families were strong, our country had a direction.*
>
> *(Source: The Los Angeles Times – 20170921-story article)*

The problem with racial confession is revealed in this candidate's answer. Apparently, he considered a terrible period of sin and ungodliness to be a great period in American history—at least for his race of white Southerners.

But was it great for the countless African slaves who were brutalized, tortured, and murdered? Was it great for the Natives who were being attacked, killed, and forced off their ancestral lands?

This is one reason America cannot truly heal. For some of our white brothers and sisters, there was not true confession—

the kind that leads to lasting change of behavior. Now, over 150 years after the official end of the confederacy, many of our white brothers and sisters still idolize and secretly long for a return to the period of pre-Civil War. Which means, there has been no realization of the true horror inflicted on minorities during that period, and no real repentance for the evils of slavery and the many atrocities against Native Americans.

When true repentance comes, so does change. And that means the evils that caused the pain, supremacy, and racism, should be firmly rejected. Unfortunately, supremacy, racism, and discrimination continue to exist and have merely taken on different forms.

Let's dig a little deeper into the Chief Justice's response. Notice the question: When was America great—not when southern white people were great. But his answer referenced a period of power, prosperity, and privilege for white people only.

Could it be that some whites think of America as a nation of whites, by whites, and for whites—only thinking of blacks and other minorities as ancillary or, worse, as foreigners who must prove their citizenship upon request?

And could such a mindset lead some white citizens to feel authorized, and even obligated, to question blacks and other minorities about their citizenship or about their right to be in certain places?

Perhaps that whites-only exclusive thinking led to several incidents caught on camera of some people inappropriately questioning minorities about their lawful presence in certain places—even escalating the situation by calling the police to investigate.

A white couple in an upscale neighborhood saw the words Black Lives Matter painted on an object outside an apartment building. They called the Hispanic resident out and started a heated confrontation, demanding to know if he lived there and asking for proof. The couple even called the police.

A black bird watcher was in a park when he noticed a white woman with a dog that was not on a leash. He asked her to put her dog on a leash. She adamantly refused and threatened to call the police and falsely report an African American man threatening her life. She called the police.

A black woman and her child were swimming at a hotel pool when the hotel staffer came out and questioned her about their presence. There were white guests at the pool, but the staffer only approached the black woman. The staffer demanded proof that they were hotel guests. Proof was provided, but the staffer still called the police.

Story after story of situations like these are abundant in America, and they suggest there are some whites who visualize America as a white nation filled with minority foreigners who are subject to proof of residency and citizenship.

The candidate also mentioned it was a time "when families were united…families were strong…" Apparently that was a reference to white families being united and strong. Such was not the case for minorities. Black and Native families were torn apart.

Family members were sold to other plantation owners for punishment or profit. Black fathers were worked from sunup to sundown and often beaten or whipped in front of their families for the slightest wrongs.

Black mothers and women were raped, beaten, and forced to bear the children of white masters. Natives were slaughtered and forcefully driven from their lands—many dying along the journey.

Was there real unity and strength in the families of slaves and natives? The candidate answered for his race only, not for every race in America.

And lastly, his reference of the country headed in the same direction was not based on true history. The country was headed in different directions: The Northern Union wanted an end to slavery and the Southern Confederacy wanted to continue in slavery—thus the Civil War.

During the slavery period, southern whites had total power, an enormous amount of wealth, and exceptional privileges and prestige, but they had to commit many wrongs to build, maintain, and revel in them.

Every one of the ten commandments that many southerners held in high esteem were consistently broken to sustain their comfortable lifestyle. Their wealth rested solely on the shoulders of the misery of black slaves—God's children who were created in His image. That is nothing to be proud of, glamorize, or consider great.

How can people confess and repent of something they still view as great?

The cure for this blindness to the need for true repentance is education. Unfortunately, both whites and blacks in southern states were taught slanted history lessons that glorified southern confederate leaders and minimized the atrocities of slavery in general.

As a result, many of our white brothers and sisters believe past confederate leaders are heroes worthy of honor and glamorization.

They also believe the rebel flag—the symbol of white supremacy and patriotic rebellion —is a part of their heritage and should be honored. But even learning the truth may not persuade them otherwise. Education only works for those who want to learn and are willing to change.

Repentance

To repent means to exhibit sorrow and regret for a mistake. When done correctly, it will usually involve the words, "I'm sorry" or "What can I do to make this up to you?"

For a person to feel sorrow, he or she must realize the magnitude of the confessed wrong. If the wrong is slavery, the person needs to realize the full impact of slavery—not just during past generations—but also upon the current generation.

Obviously, some impacts are simply not measurable. How does one measure the physical, emotional, and psychological impact of loss of homeland, culture, family ties, language, and freedom?

It would be helpful for people seeking racial reconciliation to know the details of slavery—from the capture of slaves in Africa, to the difficult daily lives of slaves on American soil.

As a young child, I was taught to not only say "I'm sorry," but to also express the reason for my apology. That made the admission more impactful for the victim. I had to really think about my actions and how they negatively impacted others. I had to focus on the details of their pain.

That mental exercise was always difficult and emotional, but the journey helped me to never commit the same wrong again.

Such a mental journey could be helpful for racial reconciliation. Whites should research and learn how Africans were captured, purchased, and stored for shipment to the various countries.

It is important to ask the tough questions and face the uncomfortable answers that follow. What were the conditions aboard slave ships, and why did so many die along the voyage across the Atlantic Ocean? How were slaves processed and sold after arriving on American soil? What tactics did slave owners use to "break" Africans and mold them for plantation use? What types of punishment were inflicted on slaves who did not conform or comply?

Gaining these insights can bring more understanding and empathy to the plight of those in the slavery period and perhaps assist in understanding the continued struggle that so many blacks still have today.

True repentance should keep the focus on the actions of self and not the actions of others. Not all white people are descendants of slave owners. For those who are, it is a good idea to repent for ancestral wrongs and resist pivoting to the role African leaders played in the slave trade. Their actions do not minimize or justify the actions of European slave traders and American slave purchasers.

Today, more than a century after the slave trade ended in Africa, there is still a bitter divide between the descendants of slave traders and the descendants of slaves. The subject matter is so sensitive that most people do not discuss it openly. But small steps are being taken to educate the public about the true events of the slave trade and to bring some sense of peace and unity to the African people.

The same must take place in America. We must face the ugly truth about slavery. Cry if we must, and even curse if that helps to alleviate the pain. But in the end, we need to be healed, united, and made free from anger and hatred.

Forgiveness

Forgiveness, in a biblical sense, means paying someone's debt who cannot afford to repay. The debtor decides to take the loss and tear up the bill so there is nothing between the debtor and payee to cause friction in their relationship. The debtor says, "I will absorb the loss just to keep peace between us."

There is a story in the Bible that demonstrates this concept. It is commonly called the parable of the unmerciful servant (Matthew 18:21-35).

In summary, the King forgave the enormous debt of one servant. But that same servant refused to forgive the small debt a fellow servant. In the end, the King punished and scolded the servant for failing to forgive as he had been forgiven.

When we apply this forgiveness model to the slavery era in America, we can say blacks are the payees and some whites whose ancestor's owned slaves are the debtors

When it comes to repaying the debt of slavery, some whites and some blacks do not have the capacity to totally repay. The debt of slavery involves so much more than any financial or material compensation could ever cover. How does one repay someone for the loss of family, culture, language, and freedom? There is no way to cover it all.

Therefore, blacks have two choices when it comes to forgiveness. They can demand repayment from whites which they will never receive and will lead to endless conflict. Or they can tear up the debt owed them and declare the bill paid in full, which is forgiveness in a nutshell.

But forgiveness for many blacks in America proves to be extremely hard. Feelings of anger and hatred are still prevalent, and some have even vowed to never forgive. Still others have managed to reach deep down into their consciences and settle the pains of the past to bring peace into their lives. For those who are still struggling, it may help to understand why forgiveness is so difficult.

We fail to Deal with the Hurt

It is natural to avoid unpleasant things. We may not want to come face-to-face with the powerful emotions attached to an incident—including horrible incidents that occurred with our ancestors. Those crippling feelings of helplessness, shame, and embarrassment tend to be too overwhelming to sort through. But it is critical that we deal with the hurt by facing the facts of the incident and asking important questions.

We misunderstand forgiveness

Misunderstandings about forgiveness can leave people chained to anger and hatred. Forgiveness does not let the perpetrator off the hook. Forgiveness does not mean that what the person did doesn't matter. The effects are real and long lasting, but forgiveness brings freedom from the negative impacts and makes room in the human heart and mind for healing. Forgiving others sets the stage of personal release from bondage. When a person says, "I forgive you," it equates to saying, "I forgive you and I release me."

Forgiveness involves a long process

For some, dealing with the pain may become a life-long process. Once forgiveness is granted, the person must live in a manner that reflects forgiveness toward others. This includes treating others with respect and kindness. If the person believes in faith, constant prayer, and asking God to grant wisdom and a change of heart becomes a process, and this process can be an extensive and difficult journey.

Release the person from any debt they owe.

It is human nature to want an apology from offenders and to expect them to make amends for what they did. In a perfect world, they should. However, personal healing should not rely upon the actions or inactions of others. At times, personal healing must come from personal actions. As already discussed, forgivers should tear up the debt and release offenders from anything owed—including an apology.

For African Americans, forgiveness for slavery and for current racism is paramount to emotional, psychological, and mental health. But forgiveness does not mean justice is no longer a desire. Blacks must continue to seek justice, equality, and a place among American society that values them for their intelligent and creative abilities.

Nine: Self-Evaluation & Discussion

Why is forgiveness so important when it comes to racial healing? Have you had something bad happen racially?

Why is being truthful so important when it comes to racial healing?

Do you sometimes perceive things or people to be about race when they may not be about race? Care to share?

What other points would you want to group-discuss in this chapter?

CHAPTER TEN

RACE and CULTURAL DIVERSITY

D iversity is a human need. I want to share a personal childhood experience that demonstrates this truth.

In my pre-teen years, I was haunted by one object in our house. It was a small mirror. I hated it because I disliked the rich-dark face that stared back at me.

Psychologists have a term for this mental condition. They refer to it as self-loathing. It is a condition where a person may constantly compare himself or herself to others only to point out perceived defects about himself or herself. It can lead to extremely low self-esteem and other issues. I struggled with this for years without knowing the cause.

One manifestation of my low self-esteem was extreme stuttering. When speaking in public, especially in front of white people, I could not complete one short sentence without slapping my leg. That was funny at age six, but not at eleven or twelve years old. Teenagers can be brutal.

I believe the onset of my self-loathing occurred due to my surroundings during the Jim Crow era of the South. As a young impressionable boy, everything in my little segregated world screamed one constant message: blacks are inferior!

Living in a segregated and poor neighborhood, most black-owned things I saw were dilapidated, deteriorated, or dirty. The water fountains, restrooms, school buildings, and even the houses of worship were inferior compared to the same things owned and used by whites in the community.

As a result, I internalized what I saw and equated the filth around me to who I thought I was—poor black trash incapable of nothing great.

As a six-year-old with a vivid imagination, I often pretended to be Superman. I loved his cape but could not afford to buy one. I made a cape by tying my older brother's long sleeve shirt around my neck. I ran around the yard and leaped over huge rocks, looking back at my cape as it danced in the wind. "I'm superman!" I yelled.

When my young black neighbors saw me running around the yard, they rushed over.

"Hey! One of them yelled. "What are you doing? Who are you supposed to be?"

I stopped saving the day for a moment, tossed the cape behind my back, and struck a power-pose before making the announcement.

"I'm superman!" I thundered. "The world's greatest super-hero!"

Silence. They looked at each other. They looked at me. "Ha! Ha!"

They all burst into thundering laughter and bellowed over from the pain in their stomachs.

"Boy! What's wrong with you? You can't be superman. Superman is white! You black! There ain't no black superheroes! Ha! Ha!"

They laughed me to shame as I slowly eased into the house.

Five years later, after I integrated an all-white school, the teacher wanted the class to learn about politics. He collected names of students who wanted to run for class president and vice president.

"Yes!" I cheered as I pumped my fist in the air. I gladly submitted my name for class president and immediately ran to my first group of "supporters": my black classmates.

"Hey ya'll!" I blurted out as they sat outside during play period. "Guess what? I'm gon run for class President!"

Again, I struck a power-pose anticipating applauds and congratulations. Instead, I got silence. They looked at each other. They looked at me.

"Ha! Ha!" They cried laughing. "That's real funny!" One of them said in between gasps.

"Boy, you can't be President cause all the Presidents are white! You black! There ain't no black Presidents!" Again, they laughed me to shame.

But this time I wanted to have the last laugh. So I campaigned, talked to white students, shared my ideas, and when the voting was done, I won..........Vice President. My white friend won President.

Sadly, I concluded they were right all along. Maybe black people were not meant to be great or do great things. I lived with that inferiority complex for years.

But one day I heard a voice on the radio. It was the unique voice of a black man speaking about civil rights. His words were elegant and powerful. He said things like,

> *"The arc of the moral universe is long, but it bends toward justice!" (Martin Luther King Jr.)*

His presence. His demeanor. His words of wisdom and his unapologetic attitude about being black made me rethink my negative view of myself. He was what I needed to see, hear, and emulate. Each time I listened to or saw him, I imagined myself speaking as he spoke, with power and passion.

I got over my self-loathing because I saw what every human being needed to see: someone who looks like him or her, doing great things and setting good examples.

I often share this story with organizational leaders to make a powerful point. Diversity is a Human Need.

Unfortunately, some leaders view diversity as a:

A necessary evil with no company benefits.

A cultural trend forced on organizations.

A popular minority equality tool.

Yet another government quota requirement.

But truthfully, diversity has always been a deep need of everyone, regardless of race. All people need to see a physical representation of someone who looks like themselves in high places doing great things.

Natives
Caucasians
African Americans

Mexicans and Hispanics
Asians
Europeans
Middle Easterners
And all others need to see diversity.

Therefore, when you as an organizational leader recognize, celebrate, and honor diversity within and among your teams, you are providing a deep psychological need for everyone: The need to see themselves in the world around them.

Race and Cultural Diversity

Several years before writing this book, I worked for a good company. The diversity present at that organization was rich with several races and cultures working side-by-side. I had never collaborated with so many different people. I took the opportunity to learn from and observe the unique perspectives that manifested on many occasions.

I worked beside Asians, Middle Easterners, Mexicans and Hispanics, Guatemalans, Caucasians, and African Americans. Although the work environment was overflowing with diversity, unfortunately, the company itself did little to capitalize on and recognize the strength of that diversity.

It was what I call a traditional organization in the sense of, "We don't talk about three things: Race, Religion, and Politics (RRP)."

For example, the company had two employee events per year: Thanksgiving and Christmas celebrations. I loved them both. But I did notice there was nothing in those celebrations to recognize or honor other races and cultures represented in the company.

The company never mentioned the strong diversity we had and never demonstrated its regard for the value of those unique cultures. There was nothing about diversity or the value of other cultures in its communications: website, email, newsletters, and business meetings. Race and diversity were never mentioned publicly.

One would think the company did not value diversity because it said it did. But I happened to know they did based on private conversations with some leaders. Perhaps the leaders were fearful based on the traditional avoidance of RRP.

Reaching hiring quotas, placing diverse people on the payroll, and appearing diverse on company reports, is not TRUE diversity. That is having diverse appearance only without having diverse functionality. Diverse appearance only is suitable for meeting diversity quotas, minority advertising, and gaining certain governmental contracts. But it is far from diverse operation.

The killing of George Floyd has left business leaders searching for ways to improve diversity and racial awareness. Now comes the difficult part: Openly discussing race, privilege, and prejudice.

As a former farmer, I understand the importance of preparing the ground before planting. When it comes to building racial diversity, the first exercise should be focused on mentally preparing attendees to embrace and engage diversity and equality.

The best way to do this is by doing antibias training before openly discussing the tough topics related to racism. This is necessary to help individuals embrace and engage in conversations while being aware of their own biases.

The steps I recommend for enhancing racial diversity are:

Communicate Diversity

Talk about it. People will never know diversity is important to your organization unless it is communicated in various ways.

From organization leaders and executives at meetings, conferences, holiday gatherings, company updates, etc.

Through various electronic means such as email, texts, newsletters, special announcements, etc.

On various social platforms such as company websites, blogs, newsletters, and many other social media apps.

Talk about it. Explain how racial diversity will build stronger teams and increase the bottom line of the organization. Celebrate it when you have various events. Teach your people to value it and in turn, seek to do their part to build unity around diversity.

Sometimes, leaders need to repeatedly emphasize "different is good" to counter the popular mental perception that different is bad.

Make a Long-term Commitment

Commit to long-term antibias training complete with a budget line item that has designated personnel, resources, and time. Bias is something that is continuously built over time and cannot be instantly plucked out of the mind. Locate and identify good antibias training programs, authors, and speakers, and exercises your organization can use to reinforce the positivity of racial diversity.

Create a Welcoming Environment

It can be challenging to get people to freely talk about tough conversations like race. Leaders and employees must feel they can open up without backlash or negative consequences. Employees need to know that what he or she shares from pure honesty will not be held against him or her in terms of performance reviews and other work-related areas.

The goal of antibias training should not be to force beliefs on individuals, but to help people become more racially aware so they can make better decisions on how to engage with others.

Develop Rules of Engagement

As rewarding as racial diversity can be, there are lines that can be crossed when people engage. That creates a need for rules of engagement such as be respectful, pause for time out, and set a time limit for each speaker. A moderator may be needed to help facilitate the discussions and make sure everyone stays on topic.

Determine Progress and Needs

The age-old leadership rules of know where you stand and know what you need are time proven to be true. When it comes to racial diversity, organizations need to know where they stand and know where they need to improve. But that takes open communication and the willingness on behalf of leadership to engage in uncomfortable topics.

After engagement, use various forms of feedback such as surveys, polls, questionnaires, and written and verbal responses.

Set Clear Learning Objectives

Set goals for in depth understanding of racial bias and its sources. Some goals could be to identify specific racial biases some employees may have. Address mental obstacles to discussing racial diversity. Provide tools and techniques for daily bias identification. Use persuasive speech to encourage an "embrace" and "engage" mindset.

Give People Diversity Freedom

It is important for organizational leaders to expressly give people what I call diversity freedom. For example, let people know, under certain circumstances, that is okay to wear their native clothing in certain circumstances.

For example, to a private company event or on free-for-all Fridays if they do not meet with customers. The same with speaking their native language. Let people know it is okay if done according to company guidelines. Explain why that might be disruptive if done in a business meeting where some people may not know the language.

When leaders give people more freedom, they should also give guidelines and examples so there are no misunderstandings.

Keep going!

Budget for antibias training every budget cycle if possible. It can be tempting to stop when racial diversity and inclusion seem fine. But bias influence employees are subjected to on TV, on social media, and in their personal lives never stops and could influence them at any moment.

I believe it is now or never regarding racial healing. Now that racial diversity has the world's attention, what will we do? Will we forge ahead through unpleasant encounters and difficulties to create racial healing? I believe we will.

***

The Challenge of Company Culture

In my nearly thirty-years of professional business experience, I've witnessed company cultures that were created in one of two ways: by Assimilation or Collaboration.

I've shared in a previous chapter about the damage of forced assimilation, but what does assimilation have to do with company culture? I will explain.

While interviewing over my career, I've often heard these phrases from interviewers:

"We are looking for someone to fit into our culture."

"We need someone who will buy into our culture."

"We are seeking someone who fits in. "

These statements follow the long-used business philosophy where leaders formed the culture they wanted and searched for people who fit that predefined cultural model.

That cultural model was much like a jigsaw puzzle complete with hard defined boundaries and pre-shaped pieces. Like a puzzle, each person has a specific place where he or she fits. When one person or piece of the puzzle leaves, the leaders search for someone who can be molded into the same shape and fit in.

While every company needs policies, guidelines, and rules, the culture does not need to be limited by unnecessary hardline predefined boundaries. That tends to lead to an assimilation mindset where employees may feel their appropriate native expressions are not welcome in the company culture.

A hard unnecessary boundary may be:

Discouragement of speaking in a native language under any circumstance.

A firm dress code limited to American (European English) culture.

No recognition or celebration of diversity or inclusion.

Unwritten expectation that employee success depends on fitting in. Thus, employees may attempt to mask things they think may not coincide with company culture even though those things may benefit the organization.

I've been there several times in my career. I've worked for companies whose leadership was so strict and firm about fitting in that I constantly walked on eggshells. There were times when I questioned my appearance, my professional opinion, and even my responses because I wasn't sure if they fit in.

I constantly watched my leaders because I knew they would not have become leaders if they didn't fit in. I took note of how they dressed, the way they interacted with others, and how they conducted meetings all to clone them. After all, so I thought, I must be just like them if I want to succeed in this company. I cannot be myself. I must change and fit in.

Sometimes, that is what a fit-in expectation does—it unintentionally creates a workplace environment where people are encouraged to:

Dress like
Speak like
Interact like
Think like
And be like others.

That is assimilation—the centuries old belief that everyone must be the same to collaborate and operate efficiently.

In contrast, I've also worked in a few companies whose culture was built on collaboration alone and had what I call an "open" culture. Those companies taught and gave guidance and freedom in areas such as:

Appropriate time to speak a native language.

Appropriate circumstances to wear native clothing.

They constantly recognized and celebrated diversity.

They encouraged employees to be themselves.

These company leaders did not use the phrase "fit-in" to our culture. They used phrases such as "enhance our culture" or "add to our culture." Both phrases give employees the impression they can be unique, genuine, and still be a valuable part of the organization's success.

Over my career, my best work and brightest innovative ideas occurred when I worked for companies with an open culture environment. They had policies, rules, and guidelines, but they didn't have hardline predefined cultural borders like a jigsaw puzzle. I witnessed vastly diverse teams come together and achieve some amazing accomplishments.

My advice is to have antibias training first, formulate the guidelines with leadership, and end with implementation. That way there will be less pushback because people have gone through training and know what to expect in terms of future diversity endeavors.

Who says people must be the same to be productive?

Functional Diversity

Years ago, I worked with two Chinese coworkers at an organization with a large amount of diversity. However, the leadership and company policies reflected a closed diversity culture with the motto of "fit-in." Most of us worked in divided cubicles with semi-privacy but could overhear conversations around us.

One day, two Chinese employees in the next cubicle were having a casual conversation about their families. They spoke some sentences in English and others in their native Chinese language. I could hear them because I was in the cubicle next to them, and so was another male employee.

I thought their conversation in Chinese was beautiful and appropriate given the circumstances. I was amazed at how fluently they changed from English to Chinese. But my male coworker had a real issue with it.

"I don't like it when they do that." He confided to me.

"This is America. Speak English so everybody can know what you are saying."

I shook my head and grimaced at him. "Oh man, just relax. They aren't talking to you, and they aren't talking to customers."

This is an example of diversity on paper but not in functionality. I'm sure that organization met its diversity hiring goal and probably seemed impressive on diversity reports. But in terms of operation, diversity was not expressly welcomed, valued, or recognized.

What that company needed was to go beyond diversity in hiring practices and create diversity freedom by having antibias training and developing diversity guidelines for employees to freely operate in their various native expressions.

Diversity should go beyond workforce and into other aspects of the organization. Diversity should be a consideration in the following areas:

Customers
Clients
Vendors
Community Outreach
Partners
And other areas.

Here are some examples of diversity guidelines.

Inappropriate times to speak a native language are:

In the presence of customers or clients who do not know the language.

In a group of people where some may not know the language.

When discussing company issues in an open area where you might be overheard.

Appropriate times to speak a native language are:

In casual or private nonbusiness conversations between two or more people where all individuals know the language.

At the need or request of customers or clients who may not be familiar with the common language of English. At such times, please interpret back in English for those in the group who only speak English.

An example company statement:

> *"Our organization has a rich representation of diverse races and cultures. As a result, we issue these guidelines as encouragement for all who wish to communicate in their native language at the appropriate times. We are convinced that making room for freedom of native expression will enhance our company culture and will benefit everyone in the end."*

The same type of guidelines can be issued for native dress and other aspects of expression. Freedom should always come with guidelines. When those guidelines are followed and people take advantage of the freedom, it will become clear that your organizational culture is not based on assimilation, but collaboration through an open culture philosophy.

Ten Self-Evaluation & Discussion

If you work for an organization, does the culture resemble that of a closed culture or open culture?

Do you think employees should have the freedom to express their cultures at an appropriate time and place? Why or Why not?

Think about the different aspects of your organization and determine if diversity is needed. If so, what can you do?

What other points would you want to group-discuss in this chapter?

CHAPTER ELEVEN

SUMMARY and CALL to ACTION

A black guy spoke to a conservative white audience about race. He did not get heckled or shouted down. Instead, he received a standing ovation!

"I have never heard anyone talk about race the way you do!" One white attendee said to the speaker.

"Everybody in the world needs to hear that speech!" An elderly white woman told the speaker.

Currently, that is hard to believe but is true. I know because I was that speaker. It was nerve racking for me and the leader who invited me to speak. Neither of us knew how the audience would react to a speech on race. But we both chose courage over fear, and it paid off.

After the overwhelming positive response, the leaders and I started work on custom race training for their organization to be delivered in early 2022.

How did I do it? I delivered the speech around four principles:

I focused more on the beauty of race, not the ugly of racism.

I zoomed out beyond the 400 years of American history to make race a human issue, not a black and white issue.

I used balance, not blame. The lesson is more important than who did wrong.

I ended with an inspirational real-life racial story to show the audience how race relationships should be.

I realize all my race speeches may not turn out as well as that one. But I refuse to give in to the fear and intimidation that often leaves race relations in shambles. I choose to be brave. Will you choose it also?

✳✳✳

Summary and Call to Action

In the introduction, I shared the four points of this book.

One. Racism is not about skin color alone. It is a character sickness with roots that are colorless such as pride, greed, selfishness, and hatred. I provided many personal stories, examples, and research to support that point.

Two. ALL people, including blacks, are subject to supremacist, racist, and biased mindsets, attitudes, and conduct.

Three words were defined and contrasted to form the foundation of that point: supremacy, racism, and unconscious bias.

I also shared several personal stories of black racism along with personal recent accounts. I believe those additions brought more balance to this version of the book.

Three. There are specific challenges that all races need to confront to help heal the racial divide. The challenges I shared are:

White Challenge #1: Acknowledge the truth about the Confederacy.

White Challenge #2: Become involved in social justice.

White Challenge #3: Practice all the gospel.

Black Challenge #1: Create a safe place for racial conversations.

Black Challenge #2: See whites as individuals.

Black Challenge #3: Open the umbrella of justice.

Black Challenge #4: Acknowledge black racism.

White and Black Challenge #1: Forgive from the heart.

White and Black Challenge #2: Rock the church boat!

White and Black Challenge #3: Acknowledge race cards.

All Races Challenge: Stand up to Racism.

Four. This is a book of SELF reflection written to lead you, the reader, into a place of pondering and evaluating yourself as it relates to racial issues.

Self-examination sections with questions to ponder and suggested discussion topics were added after each chapter to encourage self-evaluation. In the end, you and I are powerless to change others, but we can change ourselves.

Throughout the book various ideas and concepts were shared such as:

The two major hurdles of racial healing: guilt and unforgiveness.

A breakdown of systemic racism with historical and current accounts.

A biblical study on what the Christian faith teaches about race and how some scriptures have been misinterpreted and misused to support racism in America and around the world.

An explanation of the Assimilation Mindset along with historical accounts on how forced assimilation damaged and destroyed native cultures in America and around the world.

Business consultation and ideas on how to enhance racial diversity based on collaboration and open culture.

Techniques and tools for racial communication, racial unity, and racial healing.

Now, I want to end this book with one last word:

"Whitewashed."

Over two-thousand years ago, Jesus angrily addressed a crowd of Israelites. The targets of his scorched words were the religious leaders of his day. Despite the leaders' status of godly men and pillars of the community, Jesus lashed out at them and practically condemned them all.

He branded them with the label, "whitewashed tombs filled with dead men's bones."

> *"Woe to you, teachers of the law and Pharisees, you hypocrites! You are like whitewashed tombs, which look beautiful on the outside but on the inside are full of the bones of the dead and everything unclean. 28 In the same way, on the outside you appear to people as righteous but on the inside, you are full of hypocrisy and wickedness." (Matthew 23:27-28)*

It was a scathing description of powerful men who had the authority and means to have him put to death. But what did Jesus mean by the word whitewashed?

Understanding this is pivotal to knowing why we still struggle with racism in America and around the world today.

The concept of whitewashed means to cover, conceal, or hide all that is bad with a coat of paint to create the perception of beauty. It is all about appearance.

Outside means what everyone can see: dress, materialism, and positions. Inside means who we really are: our thought life, character, and mindset.

The religious leaders in Jesus' day were obsessed with their outer appearance because they wanted everyone to think highly of them. They did many things to appear as godly individuals worthy of admiration and accolades.

Everything they did, Jesus said, was done to be seen by others.

They wanted the reputation of being godly, but they failed to do the very things that godly people should do.

They failed to show compassion and mercy on the least of those people under their care.

They failed to show justice and equality in rendering their religious judgements between individuals. Instead, they stacked the deck in favor of the rich and well connected.

They were filled with ungodly pride, arrogance, and indifference to the sufferings of their own people.

They embodied all the four pillars of racism discussed in chapter one: ungodly pride-arrogance, fear-hatred, lies-ignorance, and passivity.

Jesus even told them how to fix the problem: clean the inside of the cup first.

"Woe to you, teachers of the law and Pharisees, you hypocrites! You clean the outside of the cup and dish, but inside they are full of greed and self-indulgence. 26 Blind Pharisee! First clean the inside of the cup and

> *dish, and then the outside also will be clean."* (Matthew
> 23:25-26)

Jesus used the word "hypocrite" many times concerning them—meaning one wearing a mask and who pretends, much like an actor playing a role.

Anyone can whitewash. Whites, Blacks, Asians, Hispanics, and others can whitewash their race, their culture, and even their history.

Unfortunately, the United States continues to battle with whitewashed history regarding slavery and racism. There are constant attempts to conceal, cover, and rewrite history itself spearheaded by those who do not want to face the ugly truth about their race and about America as a nation.

They rather present the whitewashed version of America instead of the real version—the good and the bad.

Here are some examples of whitewash:

The truth about the Transatlantic Slave trade was not accurately relayed in some history books and totally omitted in others.

The truth about the real reasons and occurrences of the Civil War was not put in many southern history books. Whitewashed versions of history such as The Lost Cause, mentioned in a previous chapter, were taught, and widely believed.

The truth about Native Americans was not told or communicated in public schools for some time. Haunting occurrences such as the Trail of Tears, the massacres, and the swindling of land from many Natives by some white lawyers were omitted or mildly mentioned in history books.

Minority American contributions and accomplishments were omitted from history books and often from recognition in society. The minority:

Inventors
Business Owners
Physicians
Lawyers
Authors and writers
Poets and Scholars
Soldiers and Military Leaders
And others were not acknowledged, and their rightful honors bestowed.

Even some white people who went against the norm of racism during the antebellum period of the South were whitewashed out of history by those who controlled public and private education.

For example, Robert Carter III is a name that should have been in every American history book that recounted the antebellum period and discussed slavery in America. I view him as the greatest slave liberator in American history prior to the civil war and emancipation. Yet very little is known about him or his great act of slave liberation.

Robert was an extremely wealthy Virginian whose grandfather owned massive wealth, land, and slaves. Eventually, after the death of his grandfather and father, Robert inherited the land and slaves.

But unlike his grandfather and father, Robert hated slavery. He has been described as a religious wonderer but had a Baptist background. He firmly believed slavery was immoral.

After inheriting the massive wealth and slaves, he put a plan in action to set 452 of the 455 slaves he owned, along with any children they may have, free.

On September 5, 1791, Robert delivered his carefully written and airtight legal document called "the deed of gift" to the local courthouse. The deed contained the names of 452 slaves and schedules upon which each of them would be set free.

Because slavery was the engine of the south, there were laws that governed manumission or the freedom of slaves. One of the aspects of the laws was the number of slaves that could be freed at any given time.

Robert knew the manumission laws of his area and wanted to make sure his deed of gift would stand any challenge in court. Therefore, he set the freedom schedule carefully, setting free about fifteen adult slaves per year as their children remained on his plantations.

The freed slaves were allowed to stay on and work parts of his land in exchange for payment. That arrangement allowed families with children to stay together.

Robert went far beyond freedom. He assisted the freed slaves in many ways including with loans of money to pay for manumission court costs. He also purchased items they sold as they became established.

He taught them about business and other aspects of life to help them integrate into society. And he allowed them to choose their own first and last name instead of branding them with his family name.

The process he set in place took over thirty-years to complete and eventually freed between 500 and 600 slaves. But it gave them more than freedom. It gave them a new life as most of them became productive citizens with good educations, respected occupations, and a considerable amount of wealth themselves.

His action was not without opposition. His deed was challenged by his own son and other family members, by some in the community, and by the society in which he lived.

As you can imagine, he was not a popular person among slave owners and people of society in his day. Despite the threats, shuns from people, and isolation from the social elite, Robert followed his heart. He did what was right when it was very unpopular and dangerous.

In the gift of the deed, we find Robert's reason for doing what was right. He wrote:

> *I have for some time past been convinced that to retain them in Slavery is contrary to the true Principles of Religion and Justice and that therefor (sic) it was my duty to manumit them.*

His great act of manumission for so many slaves disproved, dismantled, and destroyed the false fears used by some to keep slavery intact.

False-Fear #1: If slaves are freed, they will exact revenge on whites.

It was not recorded where any freed or current slave attacked Robert or anyone else in his family. In fact, Robert was very well liked among his slaves because he was very generous to them and often handed out a regular ration of food and meat.

Robert's children's tutor once wrote in his diary:

> *I make no Doubt at all but he is, by far the most humane to his Slaves of any in these parts! Good God! are these Christians?*

False-Fear #2: If slaves are freed, they will become a menace. They cannot integrate into society.

As evidenced by historical documents, many former slaves became very productive members of society with well-respected occupations. Some became business owners, landowners, and independent citizens who contributed to society around them in many ways.

False-Fear #3: If slaves are freed, the economic engine of the south will collapse.

Robert remained a wealthy man until his death despite the manumission of his slaves. Many of his former slaves chose to stay on his land and work with him in partnership as opposed to starting new lives elsewhere.

As a result, he did not lose massive amounts of wealth and did not die broke and penny-less as many slave owners warned would happen.

False-Fear #4: Whites and Blacks cannot live together in peace.

Robert's healthy and peaceful relationship with his current and former slaves prove this fear to be false. There is a story of two male slaves who grew impatient of waiting for their scheduled freedom. They escaped from one of the many plantations Robert owned, but they did not run away. They ran to Robert's mansion to plead with him for an early release.

Robert did what very few slave owners would have done. He talked with them and explained why it was important to wait. He gave them clothing and arranged for them to be sent back to the plantation. So no harm would come to them by the taskmaster of the plantation, Robert penned a letter, giving it to the slaves, instructing that no harm should come to them for running away.

As if that wasn't enough, Robert sent a letter by mail saying the same just in case the taskmaster claimed he did not receive the letter from the slaves.

His manumission act served as a blue-print for what mass-emancipation could have looked like after the Civil War. His acts proved releasing slaves and helping them with education, finances, and supporting their various endeavors, could work in America and lead to a healthy, peaceful, and prosperous Country where blacks and whites live together in peace and harmony.

But his blueprint of slave liberation for as many as 600 slaves was whitewashed from American history. If only his example had been followed by former slave owners after the Civil War! America could have been a vastly better place then and today.

There is a small group who still celebrate the deed of gift. They include Robert's decedents and decedents of the slaves Robert freed.

This is a story worthy of being told not just in America, but around the world. It is not just the story of another rich white man who did something good for blacks. It is a lesson in doing what was right when it was dangerous and unpopular.

Could it be that this great story of heroism and liberation is an inconvenient truth for many Americans?

Does the true story of Robert Carter III denounce the hollow elegant words of more famous men of his day who spoke about liberty and freedom but failed to free their own slaves?

After all, his slave liberation makes the excuse that "slavery was a necessary evil" nothing more than a convenient lie told by those who had no will or determination to do the right thing.

Still today, there is a great hesitancy for some Americans to talk openly and honestly about slavery and racism.

But I still love America and I continue to have hope and faith that one day we will strip away the whitewashed layer of paint and bravely face the undesirables of the past and present.

Then we will cry together, learn together, and grow together as we vow to never commit the atrocities of the past.

That is how nations mature—by owning the bad, celebrating the good, and always presenting itself as human—filled with good and bad, but always moving toward maturity.

America is a strong nation of:

Dreamers
Adventurers
Soldiers
Freedom Fighters
Experimenters
Inventors
And allies of many nations around the world.

I am fortunate to be an American citizen and to have lived in the southern portion of such a great nation.

But if this nation is to mature regarding race, it must stop the whitewashing of history and come full face with the many horrors of the past and the racism that continues today.

It is an "inside" job of character correction. The thoughts, mindsets, and opinions of many must change. Here is a photo representation in the form of a tree. The tree represents a person of any race.

Notice the bad things in the human mind located at the roots of the tree. These character issues ultimately lead to the various racist acts on the leaves of the tree.

The racist acts on the leaves need to be addressed by society and legislation but pulling off a leaf or several leaves will not stop racist acts. Remember, the roots (mind) determine what kind of leaves (racist acts) will appear.

Therefore, we want to change the overall tree but we must begin with the roots. By addressing character issues at the roots, humans can change mindsets from:

The Roots of Racism

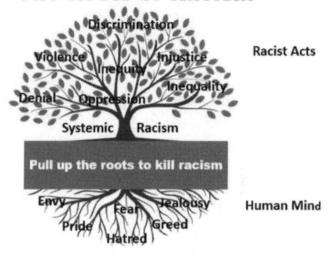

Racist Acts

Pull up the roots to kill racism

Human Mind

Hatred to Love
Pride to Humility
Envy to Admiration
Fear to Trust
Jealousy to Compassion
And Greed to Sharing.

We should not desire to uproot the tree (harm people), but change the roots so the leaves will also change. But that will take time, constant appeals to the person's good, and setting the example for others to follow.

No one can clean the inside of another person's cup or forcefully change another person's roots.

Each person only has control over himself or herself. That is the point this book makes throughout.

Please do not end this book and ponder on what someone else or some other group needs to do. This is your call to action.

What will you do with the information in this book? What will you do with the time you have remaining on this earth? Will you act in a way that makes your nation and your race better than the way you found them?

Here are some suggestions.

Commit to non-confrontational ways to defend racial equality.

Start a racial healing movement in your area.

Share the book with others verbally and in some tangible form.

Share the book with your leadership.

Suggest the book to a book club.

Ask your local library to carry the book.
Form a reading group to discuss the book.

Share the book with your faith leadership.
Invite the author to share a racial healing message with your group or organization.

Join the author's racial healing movement by registering online at SpeakerHolley.com/register.

Together, we can lead America and the world into a much-needed place of racial healing. It will not be easy and there will be resistance. But if we make a solid effort to leave the world better than the way we found it, we will succeed.

May God bless you.

May God bless America.

May God bless every nation around the world.

To read more about Robert Carter III, use this link:

https://encyclopediavirginia.org/entries/deed-of-gift-robert-carter-iiis/

Eleven: Self-Evaluation & Discussion

What actions are you taking or plan to take to help improve race relations in your country, city, or community?

Can you give an example of something that was white-washed in your personal life or history you learned?

Why is acknowledging the good and bad important to ushering in racial healing?

What other points would you want to group-discuss in this chapter?

Charles Holley Biography

Charles Holley is an International Speaker and Award-winning Author who specializes in Racial Healing, Communication, and Inspiration. He is a Race Dialogue Specialist who transforms contentious racial topics into warm conversations. He shares communication techniques that reduce racial conflict and help people engage in constructive dialogue.

His powerful and engaging keynotes and training all have three goals for organizations: Reduce existing conflict, Prevent potential conflict, and Enhance existing racial relationships.

He speaks to Corporate, School (Middle to University), and Faith based audiences. Whether speaking or writing on Racial Healing or sharing his many challenges as inspirational messages, his goal is always to make a lasting positive impact on the audience. For speaking engagements or more information about the author, visit SpeakerHolley.com.

Other Books by Charles Holley

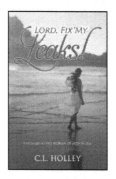

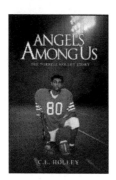

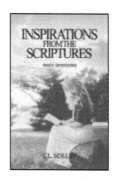

Made in the USA
Columbia, SC
11 July 2025

60329046R00135